# Fifty ways to improve your
# Presentation Skills
# in English

…without too much effort!

Bob Dignen

**Summertown**
Publishing

**Summertown Publishing Ltd.,**
29 Grove Street,
Summertown,
Oxford
OX2 7JT

www.summertown.co.uk
email: info@summertown.co.uk

ISBN 978-1-902741-86-4

First published 2007

Designed and typeset by Oxford Designers & Illustrators
Illustrated by Clive Goddard
Cover Design by Oxford Designers & Illustrators

Author's acknowledgements
To Sue, for her enduring support.



Printed in Malta

# Foreword

Do you want to feel more secure when delivering professional presentations in English? Do you want to know how to get your message across more clearly to a range of international audiences? Do you want some ideas on how to add impact to your presentations in order to influence more effectively?

If the answer to any of these questions is *Yes!* then this is the book for you!

**This is a self-help manual for those business people:**

– who have English as their second language

– who use English to give presentations

– who want to develop their presentation skills.

**You can use this book in several ways:**

• You can use it regularly as a manual to help you prepare for important international presentations

• You can read it from cover to cover as part of a self-development programme to improve all areas of your presentation skills

• You can use it as part of a wider programme to develop your intercultural competence

• You can give this book as a present to someone you know will benefit from it. (And borrow it back if you need to!)

The key words are **flexibility** and **usefulness**. You can use this book in a variety of ways. Everybody has a preferred learning style and this book is flexible enough to match yours.

Additionally, the book contains lots of very pragmatic tips which will help you communicate with your international audiences much more effectively. As a result, you will be able build better relationships and do better business.

I hope you enjoy using the book and I would welcome any feedback. You can email me at: info@summertown.co.uk.

If you have read this foreword without too much difficulty, you are at the right language level to benefit from this book.

# Contents

Also in this series:

We suggest you use the following titles with *50 Ways to improve your Presentation Skills in English*:

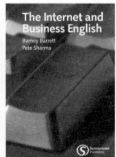

# Introduction

*'A journey of a thousand miles must begin with a single step.'* Lao Tzu

## What makes a good presenter?

Successful presentation requires both **sensitivity** and a number of **specific skills**.

**Sensitivity** is important because the style of communication has to be adapted to the specific context: to the people involved, to the subject being discussed and to the objective of the presentation. A presentation that gives information about the status of a project to colleagues will be very different from a speech at a major conference. The way we present to colleagues will be very different from the way we present to people we do not know well. So, there are very few general rules that which we can apply wherever we are, whoever we are talking to. The only real rules are to be sensitive to the context, and to adapt.

Which **specific skills** are essential to be an effective presenter? Clearly, language skills are very important, which is why this book is packed with tips on how to express what you want to say in English more clearly and accurately.

However, English language competence is not everything. As your English gets better, this begins to take second place to other skills: selecting the best content; choosing the right objective; getting the process right; adapting the language to the listener. This books also focuses on these advanced skills. Having these skills will enable you to be a truly effective presenter.

Successful presenters do two things: they **communicate clearly** and they achieve the **right impact**.

**Communicating clearly** means working hard to make sure that the audience understands both *what* is said, and *why* it is said. To make sure the *what* is understood, the message needs to be short, simple and digestible. To make sure the why is understood, the message needs to be explicit and transparent to avoid misinterpretation.

International presenters face a challenge to be clear because they are often communicating in a second language, across cultures and about very complex business processes. This book offers advice on how to be clear to international audiences.

Creating the **right impact** is about presenters knowing themselves well and knowing the expectations of their audience. They must have the flexibility to be able to achieve organisational goals at the same time as managing relationships effectively. They have to be able to engage, influence, entertain and persuade, according to the needs of the specific business situation. Again, this book gives advice on how to achieve the right impact.

## How will I achieve improve my presentation skills using this book?

The ten modules of this book provide you with a wide range of ideas and activities to help you achieve clarity and impact in your presentations.

In **Module 1** you will learn about **effective planning** using the TIPS process. Effective presenters select the right Target, Information, Process and Style for their audiences.

In **Module 2** we examine how to **structure your presentation** in order to deliver clear messages with impact.

In **Module 3** we look at how to **start a presentation** effectively. You will learn how to feel confident and make a high-impact start in the first three minutes.

In **Module 4** you will learn how to **engage international audiences**: how to deliver an interesting message with interactive techniques which can build rapport effectively.

In **Module 5** the focus is on **presentation style**. You will learn how to present with a range of styles which can be tailored to the needs of different international audiences.

In **Module 6** we take a look at **voice and body language**. Understanding how to improve how you speak and how you move is very important for international presenters.

In **Module 7 multimedia visuals** is the focus. You will get simple tips on designing clearer slides for a stronger impact. You will also get tips on how to present financial data in new ways.

In **Module 8** we will look at **closing the presentation** and **handling questions**. You will learn a number of tried and tested techniques for dealing with a range of questions more effectively. You will also learn how to deliver a clear and effective conclusion in English.

In **Module 9** we aim to give you tips to handle a number of **common presentation situations**: analysing problems, presenting a project and dealing with customers.

In Module 10 we provide you with a **comprehensive language guide** for presentations with a bank of useful phrases you can easily use immediately.

# How will I learn?

This book is an interactive learning experience with many practice exercises, quizzes and self-development questions. A key feature of the book is the **Learning diary**, a section at the end of each module. Completing the diary will enable you to reflect on your learning, to implement the techniques important for you and to track your progress using these techniques. Central to this process is the need to get **feedback** on an ongoing basis from your international audiences. It is only by being open to feedback and then acting on that feedback that you can truly develop yourself.

# What will I achieve?

Put simply, this book will enable you to make more effective presentations. It can also have a significant impact on how you communicate in other areas of your professional life. As you become more sensitive to the need to manage yourself and the communication process when working internationally, you will find that your performance in meetings, in negotiations, even in social contexts will improve and become more transparent and effective.

Good luck!

# Assessing performance

To help you start to think about your own presentation skills and the areas which you can improve, have a look at this presentation feedback sheet. If you can, get someone who attended your last presentation to complete it for you. It is through feedback and reflection on feedback that we are able to identify strengths and weaknesses, and then to develop these strengths and work on any weaknesses.

## Presentation feedback sheet

| | Poor | OK | Good | Excellent |
|---|---|---|---|---|

**Planning**

How well did the presenter plan for the specific audience in terms of ...?

| | Poor | OK | Good | Excellent |
|---|---|---|---|---|
| • the right target | ☐ | ☐ | ☐ | ☐ |
| • the right information | ☐ | ☐ | ☐ | ☐ |
| • the right presentation process | ☐ | ☐ | ☐ | ☐ |
| • the right communication style | ☐ | ☐ | ☐ | ☐ |

**Structuring**

How well-structured was the presentation?

| | Poor | OK | Good | Excellent |
|---|---|---|---|---|
| • presentation structure clear | ☐ | ☐ | ☐ | ☐ |
| • ideas developed logically | ☐ | ☐ | ☐ | ☐ |
| • effective focus on key messages | ☐ | ☐ | ☐ | ☐ |

**Starting**

| | Poor | OK | Good | Excellent |
|---|---|---|---|---|
| • How effective was the opening of the presentation? | | | | |
| • confident start | ☐ | ☐ | ☐ | ☐ |
| • benefits of presentation to audience were highlighted | ☐ | ☐ | ☐ | ☐ |
| • achieved positive impact in first three minutes | ☐ | ☐ | ☐ | ☐ |

**Engaging audiences**

How far did the presenter engage the audience?

| | Poor | OK | Good | Excellent |
|---|---|---|---|---|
| • established right level of rapport | ☐ | ☐ | ☐ | ☐ |
| • influenced audience thinking about the topic | ☐ | ☐ | ☐ | ☐ |
| • involved audience in the presentation enough | ☐ | ☐ | ☐ | ☐ |

**Visuals**

| | Poor | OK | Good | Excellent |
|---|---|---|---|---|
| • used the right number of slides | ☐ | ☐ | ☐ | ☐ |
| • designed slides professionally | ☐ | ☐ | ☐ | ☐ |
| • handled professionally | ☐ | ☐ | ☐ | ☐ |

|  | **Poor** | **OK** | **Good** | **Excellent** |
|---|---|---|---|---|

**Voice**
- speed
- volume
- was interesting to listen to

**Body language** (posture, hands, eyes, movement, face)
- looked natural
- looked confident
- added impact to verbal message

**Closing and questions**
- summarised clearly
- handled questions effectively
- concluded with impact

**Other comments about presentation style and language**

# Presentation feedback – key dimensions commentary

You can refer to modules of the book to develop any skills in those areas rated by your audiences as needing improvement.

**Planning**

Effective presenters plan their presentations in line with the needs of their audiences. (**Module 1**)

**Structuring**

Presenters need to balance structure with flexibility so they can respond to audience expectations. (**Module 2**)

**Starting**

The objectives and benefits of the presentation must be introduced with maximum impact to ensure that the audience is ready to listen. (**Module 3**)

**Engaging audiences**

Audiences will listen more closely to interesting messages, and when they feel involved in the process. (**Module 4**)

**Visuals**

Each speaker must learn to use the right number and right quality of visual supports. (**Module 7**)

**Voice**

The voice is a critical tool for the presenter. (**Module 6**)

**Body language**

Effective presenters must be both natural and convincing in their body language. (**Module 6**)

**Closing and questions**

Effective summarising, question handling and a memorable conclusion are the building blocks of an effective close. (**Module 8**)

**Other comments**

Feedback on presentation style (**Module 5**) and presentation language (**Module 10**) are also very useful for personal development.

# It's all about planning

*'It pays to plan ahead. It wasn't raining when Noah built the ark.'* Anon

Someone once said that if you fail to plan in business, then you are planning to fail. In others words, a lack of planning is likely to lead to failure. Of course, effective planning is something we always aim to do but never quite get round to. There's always a convenient distraction, whether it's that urgent business proposal to write, set of figures to submit or phone call to make. And anyway, there's usually enough time on the morning of the presentation to throw a few slides together from last year's collection of *PowerPoint* presentations.

Forget it! A presentation should be viewed as a product to be delivered to an important customer, namely, the audience. It's an offering that has to be developed very carefully to meet very specific requirements.

In this module you'll find many ideas to help you prepare that special offering, so that you can satisfy, perhaps even delight, your waiting customers, whether they are external buyers of your company's products or internal colleagues to whom you have to deliver timely information.

1 **TIPS – a new approach to international presentations**

2 **Getting the Target right**          **T**

3 **Selecting the right Information**        **I**

4 **Organising the Process**            **P**

5 **Knowing your communication Style**      **S**

# 1 TIPS – a new approach to international presentations

Some people love to plan: they love to structure, to research details, to minimise risks. Others enjoy the risks and thrills of improvisation; they work with their creativity during the moment.

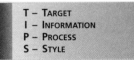

T – TARGET
I – INFORMATION
P – PROCESS
S – STYLE

The starting point for effectiveness for any international presenter is to develop sensitivity to your own approach and its potential consequences for your audience. Rate your own attitude to planning on this scale.

Ultra planner
Strong planner
Pragmatic planner
Low planner
Non-planner improviser

**ASK YOURSELF**

What are the potential positive and negative consequences of your planning style for the international audiences you talk to? For example, will they view a lot of planning as professional, or as a sign that you lack creativity?

## Planning your presentations with TIPS

TIPS is an audience-centred framework to help you prepare for international presentations. It asks four critical questions:

T  What is the right presentation **target** for my audience? What do they really want?
I  What **information** should I communicate to my audience?
P  What presentation **process** is right for my audience?
S  What communication **style** will work for my audience?

In this module we will look at the TIPS model in more detail and see how you can apply it to planning and preparing your own presentations. Remember, effective planning requires an understanding of your audience: its interests, its needs and its fears.

## Planning for your audience: a checklist of key questions to help preparation

### Background

- Who are the members of this audience?
- What are their professional responsibilities?
- What do I know and need to know about their business and cultural background?
- What does this audience think of me?

**T  Target**

- What does this audience want to hear from me?
- Why do they want to hear it?
- What do I really need to present?
- What will engage and convince this audience?

**I  Information**

- What is the audience's level of knowledge of the presentation topic?
- Which members of the audience hold strong opinions about the topic?

**P  Process**

- How do they want to hear it: in silence, interactively, or in some other way?
- How should I handle different expectations of the presentation process among the audience?

**S  Style**

- How far does my communication style match the audience's expectations?
- How can I communicate in as clear a way as possible with them?

International effectiveness depends on creating space for regular feedback which can improve performance for the future. So, remember, after the presentation you'll need to ask two more vital questions:

- How effectively **did** I prepare?
- How successful **was** I?

**ASK YOURSELF**

How could you have improved your last presentation by using the checklist of questions about your international audience?

**HOT TIPS**

- Know the advantages and disadvantages of your own planning style
- Research your audience in advance
- Ask feedback questions to help you improve for future presentations

# 2 Getting the target right

Presenters often select the wrong target or objective.
Most make the mistake of thinking they simply have to
give information. In fact, they often need to motivate, to
convince, to persuade, to listen.

| | |
|---|---|
| **T –** | **TARGET** |
| I – | INFORMATION |
| P – | PROCESS |
| S – | STYLE |

## Selecting the right presentation targets in order to achieve your business goals

Ask yourself these questions to identify your real target before you start your next
presentation. Be careful – your audience may see things very differently to you.
After identifying the right target, you'll then need to plan the content and the style
of the presentation accordingly.

Is the presentation to inform ... or to entertain?

| | |
|---|---|
| Am I here to enforce | ... or to negotiate? |
| Is my job to explain | ... or to sell? |
| Is it the time to criticise | ... or to build relationships? |
| Should I get a result today | ... or sow seeds for the future? |
| Am I going to speak | ... or to signal that I want to listen? |

## Tailoring and communicating presentation targets clearly

The opening minutes of a presentation are vital. This is when you can
communicate clearly to your audience why the presentation is important for them
and how you intend to address their needs. I often use an ABC approach to opening
presentations:

| | |
|---|---|
| Audience first! | Show an understanding of the audience's circumstances. |
| Be personally involved! | Identify with your audience personally. |
| Clear business logic | Show that the presentation objectives are based on your and their professional needs. |

Let's look at how it works. Opposite is the beginning of a presentation by a Chief
Executive Officer to senior colleagues.

*Right, I think we can get started. So, before beginning, I'd just like to say a few words about the business situation at the moment.* **Now we all know that we've had a few problems this first half year.** *And I know this has put a big strain on all of you. Many team members are worried about job losses and so managing people has become a lot more stressful in recent months for all of us.* But **I want you to know that I appreciate the good job you have been doing.** *So for today, in terms of targets, firstly, I think it's useful to clarify the financial situation of the company.* **This is a fundamental starting point and an area on which we must have clarity if we want to move forward.** *I've got the latest figures to have a look at, and these should help us talk through some possible scenarios over the next three months. Based on this, we'll also need to talk through a communication plan so that you can manage staff member questions effectively.*

Be personally involved

Audience first

presentation based on audience needs

**ASK YOURSELF**

What was the ABC of your last presentation?
What could be the ABC of your next presentation?

**HOT TIPS**

- Define a target in line with your needs and audience needs
- Plan the presentation in line with this target
- Show personal commitment to meeting the needs of your audience at the start of your presentation

**TEST YOURSELF**

1 Think of three more words for target.

   1 o.........    2 g.........    3 a..........

2 Complete these sentences with the correct verb.

   1 We should a.......... our target by the end of the month.

   2 The project has gone very well. I think we will actually e.......... our targets.

   3 Unfortunately, we have had a few problems this year so it is likely that we will f.......... to r........... our targets.

3 Complete these sentences using the verbs in the box, which you can use to introduce your targets.

   | introduce  talk  look  focus  say |

   1 I'd like to .......... on the future rather than the past today.

   2 What I want to do today is .......... at our sales channels in China.

   3 I'd like to .......... a few words about our new global leadership initiative.

   4 I'm here today to .......... our latest product.

   5 This short .......... should act as a springboard for our discussion today.

1 1 objective  2 goal  3 aim
2 1 achieve  2 exceed  3 fail, reach
3 1 focus  2 look  3 say  4 introduce  5 talk

# 3 Selecting the right information

Communication is never a simple question of transferring information. Presenters, however clear they believe they are, always face the challenge that their information will be viewed and interpreted in a number of ways by different audience members.

T – TARGET
I – INFORMATION
P – PROCESS
S – STYLE

## Getting it wrong internationally

I recently made a short presentation to a small international group in Germany, informing them of a business problem. The reactions to my presentation were quite mixed, because the various members of the audience had quite different expectations about 'information'.

The American was happy with the kind of information I gave, which was basically a brief overview of my problem with a few details. My focus was more to move quickly to a brainstorming discussion in order to find some creative solutions to the problem.

Many of the German participants were far less enthusiastic. They felt that a professional presentation had to provide a lot more background information and detailed analysis before they could offer the creative input I was asking them for.

In international business, as we can see, there are significant differences in the way in which information is viewed.

For some people, information means high complexity and precise detail; a professional should use a lot of detailed information and sophisticated analysis to eliminate risk. For others, this approach is information overload and a barrier to actually getting the job done.

Selecting the right information level for your presentation depends on understanding the different perspectives which international audiences have about 'information'. Prepare for presentations using the test below.

## Information level test

Before you select information for your presentation, rate your specific audience (5 is highest) according to what they think about four key areas: analysis, hierarchy, group and openness.

### 1 Analysis
The challenge is to balance action and analysis. Moving too quickly to action (starting a project, implementing a software) will be understood by some audiences as unprofessional. However, presenting too much data for the purpose of analysis will irritate many other audiences and could reduce commitment to your proposal.

**How far does my audience expect in-depth analysis?**      1 — 2 — 3 — 4 — 5

**How far does my audience want to move quickly to action?**  1 — 2 — 3 — 4 — 5

## 2 Hierarchy

Power structures underlie everything we do in life, and business is certainly no exception. It's essential to have a sense of your place in the hierarchy, to know what you can talk about – the content; and how you should talk about it – how critical you can be or which recommendations you are free to make. In strongly hierarchical contexts (HC) it is very important not to overstep your authority, particularly when analysing bad results or when making recommendations for change.

**How far does the context of my presentation content respect**    1 — 2 — 3 — 4 — 5
**the HC?**

**How far do my criticisms/recommendations respect the HC?**    1 — 2 — 3 — 4 — 5

## 3 Group

Audiences, and individuals within audiences, will value individualism and group identity very differently. Presenters in highly individualistic cultures may tend to give information in the form of strong personal opinions. They will be seen as professionally competent if they have clear views and communicate them powerfully.

In collectivist contexts, however, individuals will package information very differently. They may prefer to stress the 'we' and be more invisible as a personality when presenting data, to avoid accusations of self-promotion.

**How far should I sell myself when presenting information?**    1 — 2 — 3 — 4 — 5

**How much does my audience prefer 'I' to 'we'?**    1 — 2 — 3 — 4 — 5

## 4 Openness

Information to persuade others can be presented either to open up debate or to close down discussion. For example, presenters who use language such as *must, can't* or *impossible* may be seen by some as persuasive, powerful and competent professionals. On the other hand, this forceful 'packaging' of information may be seen by others to lack openness, particularly during discussion of more controversial issues. Selecting the right information 'packaging' is a key to presentation success.

**How far will powerful argumentation be seen as professional?** 1 — 2 — 3 — 4 — 5

**HOT TIPS**

- Audiences will want different information depending on their attitudes to analysis, hierarchy, group and openness
- Investigate audience expectations about information load when you plan presentations
- Some audiences may distrust data and be more convinced by presenter charisma and personality

# 4 Organising the process

A presentation can be viewed as a kind of process with specific steps, each having to be managed effectively for the presentation to be successful.

T – TARGET
I – INFORMATION
**P – PROCESS**
S – STYLE

## Step 1   The preparation

As we've seen, this phase is all about tailoring the presentation to the specific audience and business context. It's also about making sure basic logistics are in place at the venue to avoid technical disasters!

Never forget Murphy's law: what can go wrong, will go wrong. You should plan the logistics like a military operation: leave conference organisers in no doubt about your technical needs; arrive in plenty of time to test equipment (the day before if possible); have back-ups for everything, and have back-ups of back-ups! Imagine what could go wrong, and plan for it happening!

## Step 2   The presentation itself

All presentations have a beginning, a middle (with three or four parts) and an ending. For a presentation to run smoothly, international presenters need to manage five critical process factors correctly.

Ask and answer these questions about your international audience during the planning phases, particularly for larger conference events, so that you get your presentation style right.

### 1 The involvement factor

Interaction: Will my audience want to listen in silence, or to interrupt and participate actively?

Engagement: Will my audience expect to be engaged emotionally, or rationally?

Social: Will my audience want a social warm-up, or to get down to business quickly?

### 2 The organisation factor

Structure: Will my audience want a very structured or a spontaneous and creative approach?

Digression: Will my audience view digression as a lack of ability to stay focused on the theme?

Support: Will my audience see handouts as evidence of a well-prepared presenter?

### 3 Personal factor

Introductions: Will my audience expect me to start with a summary of my professional competence?

Protocol: Will my audience expect to receive my business card, possibly even translated?

Politeness: Will my audience find it impolite if I don't follow local expectations of socialising?

**4 Language factor**

Level:  Will my audience actually be able to understand the words I am using?
Voice:  Will my audience find my voice interesting to listen to?
Text:   Will my audience be helped by more or less text on the slides?

**5 Non-verbal factor**

Dress:  Will my audience expect formal or informal clothing?
Body:   Will my audience be impressed or distracted by my usual body language?
Face:   Will my audience require strong eye contact and a smile?

### Step 3   The follow-up

The presentation doesn't stop as audience applause dies down. Often this is when the really hard work begins to get your ideas implemented, to close the deal, to track the changes which you've recommended or simply to consolidate new relationships in the longer term. Make sure you plan a follow-up strategy.

**HOT TIPS**

- Learn useful phrases to help you manage the key stages of a presentation
- Prepare for audience expectations of the presentation process
- Ask someone who knows the local situation for tips on presenting there

**TEST YOURSELF**

Where would you expect to a presenter to say these phrases: at the beginning (B), in the middle (M) or at the end (E) of a presentation?

1  OK, if there are no questions on that, I'll move on. ☐

2  I've divided the presentation into two main parts. ☐

3  If there are no more questions, we can finish there. ☐

4  It's nice to see so many new faces. ☐

5  Thank you for your participation today. ☐

6  If I could just digress for a second, … ☐

7  If you have any questions, feel free to interrupt. ☐

8  Right, that brings me to … ☐

9  To sum up, … ☐

1 M  2 B  3 E  4 B  5 E  6 M  7 B  8 M  9 E

# 5 Knowing your communication style

As we've seen, understanding the way the audience thinks is vital to planning the target, the information and the process of the presentation. The final element of preparation is to know your own personal communication style, your strengths and weaknesses in front of any particular audience. In order to understand your communication style, use the tool below.

T – TARGET
I – INFORMATION
P – PROCESS
**S – STYLE**

## Analyse your own communication style

1 Circle the word in each pair which most applies to your preferred presentation style. Remember, this is not a scientific analysis. It's just an exercise to develop sensitivity to how you may come across to different audiences.

| | |
|---|---|
| distanced | personal |
| unstructured | systematic |
| formal | informal |
| complex | simple |
| indirect | direct |
| emotional | neutral |
| analysis-oriented | action-focused |
| facilitating | pushing |
| time-focused | time-flexible |

2 Ask a colleague if he or she agrees with your self-evaluation.

3 Now think where international audiences will see your style as positive, and where they could see it as negative.

4 Plan a communication style strategy for your next presentation in line with 3.

5 After your next presentation, get feedback from your audience on your style.

## National stereotypes and communication style

Stereotypes can be dangerous, but they provide useful ideas about communication style. Let's turn to a German-American culture interface as a case study[1] and look at the clash of communication styles which might occur. This could provide a German presenter with ideas on how to develop a presentation strategy.

[1] Patrick Schmidt
Understanding German and American Business Cultures
0-9685293-0-5
Meridian World Press

| German presenter style | American audience preference | German presenter strategy for American audience |
|---|---|---|
| complicated | simple | |
| detailed | concise | |
| analytical | sloganistic | This audience may see me as very serious and boring. I may need to lighten up a bit and come to the point faster than I usually do. |
| formal | informal | |
| serious | humorous | |
| factual | exaggerated | |
| reserved | personal | |
| direct + serious | direct + friendly | |

Many professionals tackle stereotyping by openly discussing the issue in order to make their communication style more transparent to others. For example, the German presenter above could use this introduction to prepare his American audience for his style of presenting, and so avoid unnecessary frustrations:

> ❝I should apologise before I start that I have a lot of statistics to go through. I know you think that Germans love statistics (*smiles*) and Americans are said to prefer action to analysis. So I will try to be as brief as possible and come to my recommendations. But I think that you will agree that it's vital to have a clear basis for any action, and I feel this requires some detailed analysis. ❞

**HOT TIPS**
- Know national stereotypes as a way of understanding how others may see you
- Think about your communication style when planning presentations
- Consider how you could adapt your style to the specific audience and situation

## How to be polite

Across cultures politeness can mean very different things. Sociologists have identified two important types of politeness: **positive politeness** and **negative politeness**. If we don't understand the politeness style of our partners, there is a risk that we see each other as impolite.

**Positive politeness** means we communicate that we like the person we are talking to: we smile, we change our behaviour, we ask a lot of questions to show interest and engagement with the person. We don't allow silence as this means the relationship has broken down.

**Negative politeness**, which is equally polite, means being more reserved, talking less, giving the other person more space and time. For those who prefer negative politeness, it is not so important to change for the other person. It is more important to just be yourself.

# Learning diary – planning presentations

## How to use your learning diary

This learning diary is designed to help you improve how you plan presentations. Photocopy it and use it regularly so you can improve over the long term. Ideally you should:

1 Complete Part 1 and Part 2 before a presentation.

2 After the presentation, ask your audience for feedback. Get their opinions on the points which you identified in Part 2 as your improvement targets.

3 Write any comments from your audience in the feedback box.

4 Use this audience feedback to identify future improvement targets for your next presentation.

Finally, maintain this learning cycle until you can't find any more improvements to make.

### Part 1: What did I learn about presentation planning in this module?

1 TIPS – a new approach to international presentations ...........................................

...........................................................................................................................

2 Getting the target right ......................................................................................

...........................................................................................................................

3 Selecting the right information ............................................................................

...........................................................................................................................

4 Organising the process ......................................................................................

...........................................................................................................................

5 Knowing your communication style ......................................................................

...........................................................................................................................

### Part 2: Which three areas of my planning will I try to improve?

Target for improvement 1: .......................................................................................

Target for improvement 2: .......................................................................................

Target for improvement 3: .......................................................................................

### Part 3: Audience feedback about my planning

### Part 4: Which three areas of my presentation planning will I improve next?

1 .....................................................................................................................

2 .....................................................................................................................

3 .....................................................................................................................

# Structuring

*'Good organisation makes things clear.'* Anon

Take a quick look around your office at your colleagues' tidy and untidy desks. It becomes clear pretty quickly that people hold very different attitudes to structure and organisation!

Across cultures there are also very different values attached to structure. Some cultures will prioritise planning and organising. Others will view this as a waste of time and prefer to get on with the job in what they see as a dynamic way and flexible way.

For an international presenter the primary objective remains to deliver a clear message with the right impact. In some contexts a higher degree of organisation will support the delivery of a clear message. When speaking to colleagues, a less structured style may be more appropriate.

In this module we examine some organising or structuring principles for business presentations which can support the delivery of a clear and effective message to both internal and external audiences.

6 **Organising principles for presentations**

7 **Making things crystal clear**

8 **Connecting ideas**

9 **Focusing on key messages**

10 **The art of improvisation**

# 6 Organising principles for presentations

When you're sitting in the audience listening to a presentation delivered in English, you are very grateful if the message is well structured. Quite simply, well-organised presentations are easier to understand. So let's review some classical ways of organising an international presentation so you can make things easier for your customer – the audience – the next time you present.

## Structuring with the business case

Presentations often use a business case as an organising principle. Here are three examples of common approaches:

**Approach 1: Proposition – Background – Challenges – Action**
Look at this structure of a presentation aiming to convince board members to set up joint venture in China.

| | |
|---|---|
| **Proposition** | Make proposal to set up joint venture in China |
| **Background** | List reasons why it's important to do business in China |
| **Challenges** | List reasons why you can't do business there without a joint venture |
| **Action** | Summarise main reasons to set up joint venture and list action points |

**Approach 2: Proposition – Negatives (problems) – Positives (why change) – Action**
This model has a different structure to achieve the same result.

| | |
|---|---|
| **Proposition** | We need to set up a joint venture to do business in China |
| **Negatives** | Problems we are having without a joint venture |
| **Positives** | Successes we would have with a joint venture |
| **Action** | Calculate sum of benefits and list action points |

**Approach 3: Attention – Need – Satisfaction – Deficit – Action**
This approach works at a more psychological level and aims to touch desires, needs and motivating factors to convince an audience.

| | |
|---|---|
| **Attention** | Get audience's attention with a creative opening – make people want to listen to you |
| **Need** | Present problem so that audience will respond strongly with the feeling 'this is not right' and 'something needs to be done' |
| **Satisfaction** | Introduce solution which audience will support strongly and enthusiastically with the feeling 'this is what I would do' |
| **Deficit** | Show consequences of *not* adopting suggested solution. The target here is to make the audience think 'If I don't do this, I will be in a worse position.' |
| **Action** | Move to action statement which will inspire trust and belief in the message, and in you as a person |

## Some more tips on structuring your presentation

Here are four common presentation contexts in business.

### Introducing the organisation

Presenters frequently use organisation charts as a structuring principle when introducing their company. But be very careful when using this approach. Such presentations can quickly become boring and run the serious risk of losing an audience's interest unless presenters integrate some analysis to highlight interesting and relevant features of the organisation they are presenting.

### Updating with the latest figures

Showing the development of a business activity over a period of time (e.g. monthly reports) with closing recommendations for action is a central organising principle for many presentations. It allows solid evidence (figures, results) to form the basis of strategic decision-making. Again, presenters need to work hard to find highlights to avoid drowning the audience in an ocean of figures.

### Comparing company locations

Sales presentations are often structured using the various locations of the company around the world:

> ❝I've structured the presentation into three main sections. Firstly, I'll start with North America, our major market and look at developments there. Secondly, a quick overview of the European sector with some highlights. I'd like to finish with two key emerging markets, Brazil and China, as I think these represent major opportunities for the future. ❞

Such structuring can allow interesting contrasts and comparisons of different departments, sites and product lines in key areas such as efficiency and profitability.

### Analysing the market

There are a number of analytical tools which provide structure to a presentation. Matrix-style formats such as the Boston Matrix, or Michael Porter's force analysis[1] are widely used to examine product portfolios or market positions. Other approaches such as SWOT (strengths, weaknesses, opportunities and threats) or STEEP (social, technological, economic, environmental, political) enable presenters to analyse significant factors affecting product and corporate performance.

[1] 'How competitive forces shape strategy' Harvard Business Review 57, March–April 1979, pp 86–93

**ASK YOURSELF**

We've already seen SWOT and STEEP. Acronyms can offer fun and punchy ways to structure messages. However, don't always rely on borrowing other people's acronyms. What acronyms could you create to communicate an interesting and engaging message for your next presentation?

**HOT TIPS**

- Develop a structure which is relevant to the content and clear for the audience
- Create individual slides with different structuring principles to ensure variety
- Think up your own acronyms to make your message memorable

**TEST YOURSELF**

Do you know the meaning of these business acronyms?

1  SMART

2  FAB

3  GROW

4  DRIVE

1  Specific, Measurable, Achievable, Realistic and Timely (used in project management)
2  Features, Advantages, Benefits (used in sales)
3  Goal, Reality, Options, Will (used in coaching)
4  Define, Review, Identify, Verify, Execute (used in quality management)

# 7  Making things crystal clear

I'm not the greatest fan of modern technologies, but one which I have grown to love is satellite navigation; to have a rather soothing voice telling me at intervals which way to turn is something I find curiously comforting. In a sense, effective presenters need to act as a satellite navigation device for their listeners. Clear speakers inform the audience at regular intervals where they've been, where they are and where they're going. Let's have a look at some navigating concepts with some exercises to practise using specific words and phrases.

### Introducing
Let your audience know with a short phrase when a new subject is coming up. This allows minds to refocus and become more attentive.

**TEST YOURSELF**

Match up the different halves of these sentences.

1  OK. Let's move …                    **a**  at the analysis of the figures from March.

2  Now it's time to turn our attention …   **b**  on to the issue of pricing.

3  Right, I think we can look …          **c**  to the question of discounts.

### Sequencing
Explicit use of sequencing language is extremely helpful for audiences to understand the structure of your message.

**TEST YOURSELF**

Complete this short presentation extract with the correct sequencing words.

> firstly   final   then   finally   secondly

OK, [1]....... , let's spend some time looking at the issue of pricing. I think we all realise that we've been feeling a squeeze on margins recently. So I suggest that, [2]....... , we look at our pricing model. [3]....... , we could take a look at the competition. [4]....... we should be in a position to take a decision about a future pricing strategy. This [5]....... point, a future pricing strategy, is what we really need as an outcome today.

**Introducing**
1 b  2 c  3 a
**Sequencing**
1 finally  2 firstly  3 Secondly  4 Then  5 final

### Connecting

After introducing a list of key points, it's useful to navigate the audience back to the list with some connecting phrases. Here are some examples:

***In relation to*** *the first point, pricing, I think ...*
***Concerning*** *the second point, discounts, I'd like to ...*
***Regarding*** *the third issue, strategy, we need to ...*

### Bridging

It's vital to create strong and logical bridges between the different sections of a presentation. We do this by managing four phases at the end of each section.

**TEST YOURSELF**

Match each phrase a–d to the correct navigating concept.

1  Signalling the end  ☐

2  Summarising  ☐

3  Asking for questions  ☐

4  Logical link forward  ☐

a  So, just to recap, the main issues here are ...

b  OK, having examined price, we now need to look at ...

c  OK, that covers everything on the issue of pricing.

d  Does anyone have any questions or comments on that?

### Developing

When you develop points to introduce new data or more complex reasoning, it can also be useful to prepare an audience with a few well-chosen phrases, for example:

*If I can just expand on that a little, ...*
*It might be useful to give a little background to this ...*

Occasionally, you might want to develop a rather unrelated or unplanned line of argument. It's particularly important to highlight any digression in order to avoid the audience making false connections with the main argument.

*If I can digress for a second, ...*
*One interesting thing, a little bit unrelated, is ...*

### Referring backwards and forwards

Very often presenters want to remind audiences of what has already been said. or postpone discussion of something until later in the presentation. There are standard phrases to navigate the audience in this way:

Referring forward:  *If I may, I'll come to that later when I talk about ...*
Referring back:  *Yes, as I said earlier, ...*

1 c  2 a  3 d  4 b

**Closing**

The final moment of navigation is at the ending of the presentation. Three important signals need to be sent here:

1 Signal the ending
2 Signal your summary
3 Signal the conclusion

**TEST YOURSELF**

Match two phrases to each of signals 1–3 above.

a In conclusion, I'd like to stress one point. ☐

b Before I close, I'd like to summarise. ☐

c Good, I think that covers everything. ☐

d So, if you remember one point from the presentation, remember this. ☐

e Perhaps a quick recap of the main points would be useful. ☐

f OK, I think that brings me to the end of the presentation. ☐

**HOT TIPS**

- Navigate your audience through your message
- Adapt the level of navigation to the needs of your specific audience
- Develop navigation phrases which you are comfortable using

a 3  b 2  c 1  d 3  e 2  f 1

# 8 Connecting ideas

Gestalt theory, from the world of psychology, suggests that the mind works by finding patterns. When faced with disorder, it produces order, creating sense from chaos by finding patterns, correlations and structures. An audience listening to a presentation is also trying to produce some form of order, to make sense, from the input.

As we have seen, presenters can support this process with clear organisation and navigation through the content. Importantly, presenters need to plan at sentence level, and to connect ideas effectively and clearly with the use of linking words and phrases. Let's look at some examples in presentation extracts.

## Linking words and phrases

**TEST YOURSELF**

1 Replace 1–10 in the presentation extracts below with a synonym from the box.

| | | | | |
|---|---|---|---|---|
| particularly | in spite of | on the other hand | due to | actually |
| for instance | as a rule | with the aim to | moreover | but |

**Adding**   *additionally, on top of this*
I think the there will be clear cost benefits in adopting the software. [1]*Additionally*, we will have a solution which is more easily upgraded in future years.

**Contrasting**   *however, whereas*
We need to spend money on the new software; [2]*however*, we must make sure that the money is wisely spent. Although huge companies such as Microsoft can perhaps afford mistakes, we can't.

**Exemplifying**   *for example, such as*
I can see a number of practical benefits to using this software, [3]*for example*, training would be much cheaper, as the program is less complex than the current one. And the use of external consultants such as Highsoft could be reduced dramatically.

**Generalising**   *normally, generally*
We don't need to upgrade the website very often. [4]*Generally*, companies of our size upgrade once every three years.

**Specifying**   *in the case of, especially*
I have heard your concerns. In the case of cost overruns, I will make sure that the agreed budgets are fully respected. I will also make sure that full user documentation is provided, [5]*especially* for trouble-shooting if the system crashes.

**Conceding**   *despite, even so …*
I sense that you are beginning to come round to my point of view on this [6]*despite* earlier concerns. Even so, you are not fully persuaded. Am I right?

**Offering an alternative**   *alternatively, on the one hand*
We have several options. On the one hand, we can go with implementation before January. [7]*Alternatively*, we could wait until the New Year and use next year's budget.

**Explaining purpose**   *in order to, so that*
I'm presenting this solution [8]*in order to* create a better foundation for our organisation for the future. We need a better IT solution so that we can expand.

**Contradicting**   *in fact, surprisingly*
I was talking to several of our competitors at the trade fair in Lyon last week and, surprisingly, it seems we are the only company in our class which hasn't upgraded. [9]*In fact*, it may be that we are the only company in France still using Windows 95.

**Explaining why**   *because of, as a result, therefore*
I believe that we have to reduce costs [10]*because of* a recent fall in orders which has led to a difficult financial situation. Therefore, I would like to present some ideas on where we can save money.

2   Complete this presentation extract using the words in the box.

| however   additionally   therefore   for example   despite |

**Making the case for an external board appointment**

OK. I can think of various cases where boards recently have gone for an external appointment to introduce fresh insight into the leadership. [1]……… , BW appointed Jocken Klansmann as their new CFO last month from Rentaud and he has already produced beneficial changes in the accounting processes. [2]……… , he has promised to support the COO with ongoing reorganisation as he has substantial experience in operations, too. [3]……… the obvious benefits, [4]……… , I know that there is significant resistance among the board to an external who would be new to the culture of the organisation. [5]……… , I would be prepared to extend the period of time we spend looking for a candidate as a gesture of goodwill in respect of these concerns.

---

**HOT TIPS**

- Structure your presentation with connecting words to support your audience
- Listen to and learn from other presenters to see how they connect ideas effectively
- If possible, ask a friendly colleague in the audience for feedback on how clearly you expressed your ideas

1  1 Moreover   2 but   3 for instance   4 As a rule   5 particularly
   6 in spite of   7 On the other hand   8 with the aim to   9 Actually   10 due to
2  1 For example   2 Additionally   3 Despite   4 however   5 Therefore

# 9 Focusing on key messages

A presenter needs to be able to focus audience attention on critical information in a presentation. Within a clear and structured framework, presenters have to highlight and emphasise the key points they want their audience to consider. There are two elements to focus on: the intention behind the message, and the key content withing the message.

## Focus on positive intentions behind the message

All international communicators need to work very hard to focus their words in such a way that the positive intention behind the message is explicit and clear.

Compare these two extracts. In each case the presenter intends a positive message, but only in the second does the presenter ensure that the audience 'hears' it.

### Version 1

**Presenter says:** *I think we need to implement this solution as soon as we can.*

**Audience might think:** *This guy is telling us what to do. We need more time to reflect and yet we have to do it as soon as possible. Obviously, he doesn't trust us!*

### Version 2

**Presenter says:** *OK, I hope you feel we have discussed the solution together in sufficient detail. My intention is not to pressure you, but really to strongly recommend a solution which benefits us all. I think we need to improve the situation and, unless you feel we need more discussion, we should go for this. What do you think?*

**Audience thinks:** *We are trying to find a common solution. We are not under pressure but very much part of the decision-making process. We are trusted and feel engaged in supporting the effort to find a solution.*

If you present your message in an implicit way, as in Version 1 above, you increase the possibility that your audience will misunderstand the motivation behind it. Minimise this risk by taking care to make sure your positive intentions are clear and explicit.

### A cultural footnote

Despite a western belief that clarity and specificity are positive values, there are many parts of the world (e.g. certain Asian business cultures) where communicating implicitly and indirectly is the norm, and where being 'to the point' and explicit about intentions may be received as an unwelcome directness, even to the point of being perceived as impolite or aggressive. As always, research your audience and adapt your style to the situation.

### Focus on key content in the message

Let's look at some linguistic strategies that you can use to focus audience attention on key points.

**TEST YOURSELF**

Match these five sentences to the correct headings below.

> a  We need to take action, and we need to take action now!
> b  Basically, we have little choice.
> c  Let's examine this more in detail.
> d  What we can't do is wait.
> e  We need to focus on one main issue here, namely, profitability.

**1 ☐ Use explicit stress**

Use verbs which signal that you are about to say something important:

*I would like to **stress** two points.*
*It's important here to **highlight** here the issue of costs.*
*I should **emphasise** that the customer is our first consideration here.*

**2 ☐ Repeat for emphasis**

Repetition is an effective way of focusing attention on core content:

*This has been a problem for a **long, long** time.*
***The more** we discuss, **the more** serious the problem becomes.*

**3 ☐ Position the core message effectively**

We tend to remember the last thing we hear. Presenters can focus their audience by placing important messages at the end of sentences, using *What* … structures.

***What we need to do is** act now.*
***What is really important to consider is** how the customer feels.*

**4 ☐ Simplify to focus**

Keep it short and simple. Many international audiences won't understand long complex messages in a foreign language.

***To put it simply**, we have two options.*
***Essentially**, there is only one viable option.*

**5 ☐ Highlight analysis**

Remind the audience from time to time to think hard about what is being said.

*What does this mean exactly?*
*Let's just take a few minutes to look at this more closely.*

**HOT TIPS**

- Make it clear that you are positive, to motivate the audience
- Highlight key content with phrases which help the audience focus
- Take your time with important content – repeat, repeat, repeat …

1e  2a  3d  4b  5c

# 10 The art of improvisation

For the more organised among you who love to plan a presentation down to the last detail, even to the extent of actually scripting what you will say, it may come as a surprise that such commitment to structure may be problematic for certain audiences. Here are some of the risks.

Your audience may see you as incompetent.

Your audience may see you as arrogant.

Your audience may see you as a slave to *PowerPoint*.

### The value of adopting a more open-ended approach

If you feel the audience would benefit from a more open-ended and improvised approach, then you need to plan and deliver your presentation accordingly. Here are three tips to develop a more flexible presentation style.

**Reduce** the number of slides you prepare. It is difficult to move flexibly around a subject if you have planned a linear delivery using over forty slides. Remember, though, that reducing the number of slides means you have to keep more content in your head, so more rehearsal is necessary.

**Use** creative slide formats. Slides with a lot of content, especially those with just bullet points, will restrict your ability to improvise your input on complex subjects. It may be interesting to experiment with more conceptual and graphically-oriented slides which allow you to approach topics from different angles, depending upon audience reactions or interest during the presentation.

**Ask** your audience questions. If you want to really tailor content to your audience, then you need to know what they are thinking, what interests them and what they know about the subject. You can do this by using an interactive approach:

- ask for a quick show of hands to collect opinions on a topic
- do short pairwork or group tasks with reported feedback in plenary
- offer plenty of opportunities for your audience to ask questions.

### When things go wrong – surviving disaster

How good are you at coping with the unexpected, the slightly inconvenient, or the downright disastrous? How far would you describe yourself as a 'disaster master'?

Look at this list of 15 potential disasters. What would you do?

1  Somebody walks in late for your morning presentation
2  The laptop crashes and won't reboot
3  A 'listener' falls asleep
4  The overhead projector begins to smoke
5  You drop all your slides on the floor
6  Somebody calls out 'Rubbish!'
7  You totally forget what you wanted to say
8  Two people get up and leave
9  The only pen for the flip chart runs out
10  The screen won't go up
11  A mobile phone rings
12  One person keeps asking you questions
13  The audience looks bored
14  You realise the pen that you used on the large whiteboard uses indelible ink
15  You look at your watch and you have five minutes left but twenty slides to go

**TEST YOURSELF**

Match the presenter comments to one or more of situations 1–15 on page 26.

a  That will be my boss. Tell her I'm on the way. ☐

b  Maybe I should recap quickly before moving on. ☐

c  OK, maybe we should move to a few questions at this stage. ☐

d  That's interesting. Why do you say that? ☐

e  Ah, good evening. ☐

f  Is there a technical doctor in the room? ☐

g  OK, if I may, I'd like to involve a few more people. ☐

h  This is not part of the plan. Just bear with me a second. ☐

**HOT TIPS**

- Don't under-estimate your ability to improvise – and the more you do it, the better you get
- Don't script a presentation – audiences may interpret this as a lack of confidence
- Don't prepare too many slides – it will reduce your ability to improvise

a 11   b 7   c 13 (2, 7, 9, 15)   d 6   e 1   f 2 (4, 10, 14)   g 12   h 2 (4, 5, 9, 10)

# Learning diary – structuring presentations

## How to use your learning diary

This learning diary is designed to help you improve how you structure presentations. Photocopy it and use it regularly so you can improve over the long term. Ideally you should:

1 Complete Part 1 and Part 2 before a presentation.

2 After the presentation, ask your audience for feedback. Get their opinions on the points which you identified in Part 2 as your improvement targets.

3 Write any comments from your audience in the feedback box.

4 Use this audience feedback to identify future improvement targets for your next presentation.

Finally, maintain this learning cycle until you can't find any more improvements to make.

### Part 1: What did I learn about structuring presentations in this module?

6 Organising principles for presentations ...............................................................

...........................................................................................................................

7 Making things crystal clear ...............................................................................

...........................................................................................................................

8 Connecting ideas .............................................................................................

...........................................................................................................................

9 Focusing on key messages ................................................................................

...........................................................................................................................

10 The art of improvisation ....................................................................................

...........................................................................................................................

### Part 2: Which three areas of my structuring will I try to improve?

Target for improvement 1: ......................................................................................

Target for improvement 2: ......................................................................................

Target for improvement 3: ......................................................................................

### Part 3: Audience feedback about my presentation structuring

### Part 4: Which three areas of my presentation structuring will I improve next?

1 ........................................................................................................................

2 ........................................................................................................................

3 ........................................................................................................................

# Making a good start

*'The beginning is the most important part of the work.'* Plato

Take a sip of water. Breathe deeply. Imagine yourself in beautiful surroundings. Perhaps you're on a beach with the sound of the ocean in your ear, the warm summer sun on your face …

All very nice but when you open your eyes you're still faced with row upon row of staring faces waiting for you to open your mouth and say something sensible. And this is when the nerves really start, the mouth dries and the knees begin to shake. The opening minutes of a presentation are often the most stressful, but are also the most important.

The next five units will give you lots of ideas to manage the opening of your future presentations more successfully.

11  **Feeling confident**

12  **The first three minutes**

13  **Objectives or benefits?**

14  **Starting with impact**

15  **Using humour**

# 11 Feeling confident

Many people fear public speaking in their own language, let alone in a foreign language. However, confident speaking is essential in a business environment. Most business presentations are designed to influence, to shape opinion and to build a platform for critical decisions. And if you are not confident in yourself and your message, then why should your audience be?

## An action plan to build confidence

Try these ideas to start your next presentation with more confidence.

### Write down the real benefits you can offer your audience
Your confidence levels will remain high if you know that your presentation has relevant and interesting content for the audience.

### Talk through with more experienced colleagues
Before you enter the presentation room, talk through the presentation with more experienced colleagues. Feedback will enrich your presentation and generate ideas and confidence.

### Remember your own competence
Remind yourself frequently that you are a specialist with more knowledge than many in the audience. Don't undersell yourself. However, don't put yourself under pressure with unrealistic expectations about what you can offer.

### Rehearse the introduction intensively
Talking through your slides is a great way to check that the main ideas are coherent and that you have the vocabulary to express yourself. But don't over-rehearse as this can reduce your spontaneity on the day. Focus on getting the introduction fluent: after the first few stressful minutes, the presentation generally goes smoothly.

### Look good on the day
Appearance is only skin deep, but you will approach public moments much more confidently if you feel comfortable with how you look. New clothes and a good haircut or new hairstyle are likely to give you confidence.

### Get physical
Take a few deep breaths, stretch a little, walk around and loosen up before you start.

### Interact with the audience before you start
Walk around and talk to people as they come into the room. Put them in a good mood and make them curious about what they're going to hear.

### Focus on the positive people around you
Most audiences are a mixed bag of the enthusiastic and the indifferent with a few aggressive types. If you need friendly faces, look for those smiling and nodding in the early stages and talk to them.

### Enjoy the tension

Anxiety is absolutely natural and totally necessary to give you that extra adrenalin rush to be an energising speaker. Start getting nervous if you're not nervous!

### Go for it

Think positive thoughts and say 'I can do this' as you stand up to begin.

### Keep quiet about your stress levels

Anxiety typically doesn't show. Your audience probably won't notice any nervousness so certainly don't draw attention to it with 'honest' admissions about nerves or excuses about your poor English.

## Frequently-asked questions about building confidence

Answer these questions yourself and then compare your answers with those of the presentation expert below.

1  How useful is it to prepare notes to accompany each slide?

2  How do I handle audience members who are more expert than me in the subject?

3  What do I do if I forget what to say?

4  How should I react if someone walks out after a couple of minutes?

5  What happens if I start to get nervous after I've started?

1  ❝I never prepare notes for each slide. Personally, I think it looks a little unprofessional if I have to read a card to remember what I want to say.❞

2  ❝If there are experts in the room, view them as a resource and not a threat. Involve them at the right time, as your audience may appreciate hearing their views. Remember, your first concern is delivering benefits to the audience, not promoting your own status.❞

3  ❝If your mind goes blank, take a few minutes to summarise what you have said and ask for questions or comments. It's always a good idea in the planning phase to have a series of back-up questions. And don't forget, pick on a friendly member of the audience to ask, if possible, to ensure that you get an answer.❞

4  ❝Let them go. They have probably got a very good reason to leave.❞

5  ❝Nerves are not necessarily a bad thing. However, if nerves do hit you, then get pragmatic. Re-focus on the content and on explaining points of interest to the audience. You can always go to your back-up questions, if necessary.❞

**HOT TIPS**

- You can generate confidence by knowing you can present benefits to an audience
- Plan back-up questions for your audience when you need to take a break
- Just in case you forgot, rehearse and rehearse, especially the introduction!

# 12 The first three minutes

Presentations with a poor opening seldom succeed. So what makes for an effective opening? Well, as with most things in life, it depends. There are a number of variables which will determine the type of introduction you should go for:

- the business context of the event (is the mood positive or difficult?); the audience (colleagues or customers?)
- the objective (motivational or pressurising?)
- your strategy (safe or sensitive?)
- your preferred communication style (formal or informal?).

Whatever the context, you need to create a first three minutes that is stimulating, clear and with the right tone for the audience in front of you. Let's look a menu of elements which you can select from to make up your own effective first three minutes. You will find suggestions for actual phrases to use on page 00.

**Welcome**   This can be anything from a simple *Good morning everyone* to *Your Royal Highness.*

**Say a word of thanks**   Presenters often need to take time out to thank hosts or organisers. A word or two of acknowledgement to the person who has introduced you is basic politeness.

**Frame positively**   Communication theorists tell us expressing positive expectations at the beginning of our message increases the chances it will be received positively. So, if you are happy to have been given the opportunity to speak on an interesting topic, say so!

**Hook**   Hooks – techniques designed to grab the attention of audiences – will be examined in more detail in the next unit. One technique is to ask a quick question which forces a show of hands – it's physical and fun. However, be aware that hook techniques, while they promise to deliver a lot in terms of audience engagement, also carry a higher risk of failure than simpler and safer approaches to the introduction.

**State objective**   It is a 'must' to state your target clearly. My experience tells me that you don't just state any objective once: in fact, you need to say it twice or three times in the course of the first few minutes so that people really get the message.

**Offer some personal information and/or reflection**   The style here may vary internationally. Some audiences may expect to hear about your professional competence. Others may want to hear about the real you, the person, the funny and loveable you! Whichever route you take, don't waste too much time if you are familiar to the vast majority.

**Show understanding of your audience**   Take the opportunity to get to know your audience and build a relationship with them.

**Emphasise benefits**   This is the great weakness of most business presentations. People are quick to talk about objectives but so often forget to sell benefits: the *What's in it for me?* factor.

**Demonstrate personal commitment**   Statements such as *I really want to* ... show commitment to and solidarity with an audience, making it more open to your message.

**Structure**   International audiences working in a foreign language will generally appreciate explicit structuring, especially at the start, to help them navigate through the content easily.

**Clarify the role of the audience**   You may want your audience to participate but, in my experience, this can be a behaviour which is difficult to stimulate. Very often people view silent observation of presenters as a form of respect. Research your audience and plan accordingly.

**Mention logistics**   It may be useful to mention various logistical factors such as timing and refreshments, particularly with smaller audiences for whom you can be more flexible.

**Link to start**   Signal clearly that your introduction is over and that you are ready to start.

**ASK YOURSELF**   Which of the above do you normally include when you present internally and externally?

**TEST YOURSELF**

Match each of the highlighted sentences in this presentation extract to one of the opening elements on pages 32–33.

'Good morning everyone. Many thanks, Peter, for your very kind words of introduction. Perhaps I should start by saying how interesting it is for me to be here at the conference. [1]The morning sessions were fascinating and I hope I can build upon what you've heard so far, and introduce some more interesting ideas to the discussion about global leadership.

[2]By the way, how many people believe they know what 'global leadership' means? OK, let me see, there are a few brave hands raised, but a lot more confused faces. So, this is my objective today, to look at the issue of global leadership, see if we can get to a definition and to some understanding of how companies can implement it across their organisations. My interest in this stems directly from a very personal need. [3]I am an HR director who was recently entrusted with creating a global leadership programme, so this whole field is very close to my heart. And I know that many of you are also struggling with this problem. Some of you have already implemented programmes and I look forward to hearing your experiences. At the end of the next ninety minutes, I hope we will all have a greater sense of the challenges facing us when trying to implement global leadership and, because you are very pragmatic people, [4]I really want to pass on some new ideas of things which you could try when you're back in the office.

So, in terms of structure, I've tried to keep it simple. I've just divided the presentation into two parts: firstly, I want to look at definitions of global leadership and, secondly, then look at how to achieve it in major organisations. [5]As there are only around thirty people here, I think we can keep it fairly informal, so please feel free to ask questions or comment at any time. As I said, we have ninety minutes and then we have a fairly long coffee break during which I hope we can continue our discussions. So, let's move to the first issue, and very challenging issue: what exactly is global leadership? '

**HOT TIPS**

- Spend more time planning the introduction than any other section
- Remember, if you want your audience to be enthusiastic about the subject, be enthusiastic yourself!

1 Frame positively
2 Hook
3 Offer some personal information and/or reflection
4 Emphasise benefits
5 Clarify the role of the audience

# 13 Objectives or benefits?

Remember, your audience is your customer. Focusing on their concerns and interests early in a presentation is a key to success. All too often presenters begin with a quick statement of the objective, a brief description of content and then rush straight to the first spreadsheet, whereas you need to invest enough time at the beginning of a presentation to convince your audience that you have something relevant for them to listen to.

Treat the audience as a customer who will be convinced by benefits or solutions to their problems rather than by listening to your objectives. Here are some ways to develop a more audience-centred introduction to your next presentation.

## Acknowledge customer problems personally and be solution-oriented

Start the presentation by showing your understanding of the solution your audience needs. If you make this understanding really personal, you will have even greater impact on your audience. Contrast the following:

**Usual start**

> ❛I'd like to talk through the figures from the last month with you. ❜

**Customer-focused start**

> ❛Now we've had some problems in the last month. I know this has been a concern for many of you, Josep particularly, so I though it would be important to look at the figures in detail so we can get things right for next month. ❜

## Tailor the content to customer needs

Presenters usually miss the opportunity when introducing the content of the presentation to show how much it has been tailored to meeting customer concerns. Contrast the following:

**Usual start**

> ❛I've divided the presentation into three parts. Firstly, product features. Secondly, comments from your technical specialists. Finally, some thoughts about future cooperation. ❜

**Customer-focused start**

> ❛So, in line with your main concerns, I've decided that it is best if I talk about product features first. We have discussed this already, but it's good to go over things to make sure you're totally happy. Secondly, the comments of your technical people have been really helpful in identifying upgrades and we should look at these. I'll end with the a few comments on future cooperation, as I feel it's important to make sure you feel confident about the product for the future. How does that sound? ❜

### Stress common interest between presenter and customer

Many of the business people I work with are from headquarter organisations. They often have to travel and make presentations which announce changes that create real pressures for subsidiary organisations. In these situations it's vital to create a sense of 'we' early in the presentation to allow ears to really open and for the message to be heard positively. Stressing joint interest and joint benefit is a simple opening strategy to build bridges. Contrast the following:

### Usual start

❝ I want to look at the project schedule to clarify a number of things: firstly, the time line and important milestones; and secondly, I want to make clear the precise results and the level of quality of these results which this project has to deliver. ❞

### Joint-interest start

❝ Today, as agreed with everyone, we feel it is important to clarify the project schedule. As you know, this project is vital for the whole organisation and will produce benefit here and in the headquarters in terms of efficiency. I think we need to focus on two areas: firstly, we need to discuss the schedule in order to have a common understanding and a common commitment to the milestones; secondly, and what is critical for everyone, to talk about the kinds of results and quality of results which we want to achieve. ❞

### Promise to answer your customer's questions

In order to deliver the right solutions to customers, we need to know the customer's problems. We get this knowledge by asking the right questions. A simple technique to show your audience that you intend to answer their key concerns and questions is to place them right in the introduction, with a promise to deliver the answer. Contrast the following:

### Usual start

❝ My objective today is to introduce the new handheld PC, which we plan to launch at the end of the second quarter this year ... ❞

### Customer-focused start

❝ Today we will be looking at our new handheld PC. And I can see the questions in your eyes already. 'Have you improved the battery life?' – which many of you were so unhappy about. 'Have you included WiFi as a standard?' – we had a lot of requests for this. 'Can you solve the compatibility problem with our ISP?' – this was the biggest request we had. 'Will I be able to use it anywhere in the world?' – this is important to many of our users. In fact, I'll answer all of these questions and many more during the course of the presentation ... ❞

**HOT TIPS**

- Your job is to present benefits not objectives
- Create customer focus right at the start of your presentation

# 14 Starting with impact

Wouldn't it be nice to be able to start a presentation with such originality and impact that you have an audience happy and motivated within the first few moments? Some people seem to do it with ease. Others spend hours planning but fail to come up with anything.

**TEST YOURSELF**

Here are some techniques for high-impact openings. Match each one with a presenter comment.

1  Make a controversial statement to wake people up ☐

2  Introduce an amusing personal anecdote ☐

3  Ask the audience a question ☐

4  Get the audience to do something ☐

5  Allow disaster to happen ☐

6  Entertain with a trick ☐

7  Find a great audio-visual ☐

8  Pair up with someone to do a double-act ☐

9  Offer prizes ☐

10  Use a quotation to make your point ☐

a  ❛Yes, I like the 'Ask your partner approach' right at the beginning. It can create a real buzz in the room and a real launch pad for the presentation.❜

b  ❛To kick off a presentation about cultural difference, I heard a guy from the UK express his shock at hearing an announcement on a Swiss train which was apologising for the train being two minutes late. In the UK this would have been cause for celebration.❜

c  ❛I taught myself to juggle in a week and performed in front of audiences just to prove that anything is possible if you put your mind to it.❜

d  ❛I was recently in Hong Kong and saw three presenters at the same conference animate their audience by showing them prizes they could win during the presentation in the first couple of minutes.❜

e  ❛This is a high-risk approach. I heard of a company CEO who strolled up to the stage to start his presentation, fell flat on his face and lay there for two minutes. The audience really didn't know what was going on until he stood up, walked to the microphone and said 'Unless we talk serious strategic change today, this company is going to fall flat on its face. And it doesn't look nice, does it?'❜

**f** ❛I've seen quite a few cases of people asking a colleague in the audience to ask pre-planned questions. It worked quite well once when the colleague pretended to be an unhappy customer and asked a series of very tough questions. The presenter used the questions to focus his audience of sales reps on the issue of customer service and the fact that they were failing. ❜

**g** ❛I once saw someone start a presentation about effective team building by asking his audience to forget everything they had ever read about team building. ❜

**h** ❛I saw a recent presentation from a big consulting company with a photo from the World Cup with the English football team in tears after the penalty shoot-out. The caption read 'Practice doesn't make perfect. Call on the experts to get results. ❜

**i** ❛I always have a few sentences from people like Albert Einstein or Peter Drucker peppering my presentations. One of my favourites is from Tom Peters. He said about managers 'If you're not confused, you're not paying attention.' I like that, because I am always confused. ❜

**j** ❛This is a technique I see used frequently, especially rhetorical questions. I even saw one guy start his presentation with the question 'Instead of listening to me, what would you rather be doing?' He went on to talk about motivation. ❜

**ASK YOURSELF**

Which three of the above techniques do you personally prefer? Why?

**HOT TIPS**

- Experiment with all of these techniques over the next twelve months
- Don't start with a joke – you may not be as funny as you think
- If you hear an amusing anecdote, integrate it into your own presentation

1 g  2 b  3 j  4 a  5 e  6 c  7 h  8 f  9 d  10 i

# 15 Using humour

I was recently at a conference waiting to hear a presenter on intercultural communication. The host began as follows:

> ❝I'd like to say a few words about our next scheduled presenter. He is one of the foremost authorities on his subject. He has written extensively on the subject and is author of several best-selling books. He is also well known on the conference circuit as one of the most engaging presenters you will find. Unfortunately, he can't be here with us today so please welcome instead John Hansen. ❞

The audience smiled, laughed and applauded as John Hansen walked on stage. Everything was set for him to deliver his presentation successfully with his 'warmed-up' audience. So humour helps. It's enjoyable. More importantly, humour can make messages more memorable.

## Ways to introduce humour into your presentations

Here are four tips to put a smile on the audience's face.

1  Use a play on words in the presentation description or title to set the tone for the introduction. You could maintain a light tone by displaying a fun visual (a cartoon or photograph) for the audience to read as it comes into the room.

2  The personal introduction is a great moment to lighten the atmosphere by making a few jokes at your own expense. For example, if you're a presenter with a long list of book titles to your name, inform your audience that you're a unique writer – you have more book titles than readers.

3  Humorous anecdotes are a favourite starting device with many presenters. These usually make fun of the presenter's own failings or mistakes as an entry point into the presentation topic.

Here is an anecdote to introduce a presentation on the challenges of communicating across cultures:

> ❝I was recently at a conference in London and I spotted this Swedish lady – I knew that from the badge – sitting alone on a sofa. She looked kind of alone so I thought, let's go socialise and make this person feel welcome. So, I went over and I started with the usual polite stuff such as 'How are you today? What did you do last night? How long are you staying? First time at the conference?' and so on. She didn't say much, so I just said politely 'You seem very quiet today.' She looked at me and said 'Yes, and you seem very noisy.' That's when I realised that English and Swedish conversation styles are very different. ❞

4  Collect and use other people's anecdotes. You get exactly the same effect if you tell someone else's story by starting *Somebody once told me about a time when they …*

**A word of warning**

Be careful with playing the role of incompetent. It's easy to overplay it and for it to be seen as a form of false modesty. Additionally, this form of 'laughing at oneself' may be more common in some business cultures than others. As ever, research your audience.

**Quotations**

Quotations are a great way to introduce clever, humorous and very relevant insights on a number of business topics. You can find useful quotations on these websites:

http://en.thinkexist.com

http://quotations.about.com

http://www.wisdomquotes.com

Enjoy the samples below by testing if you know who said what.

1  On leadership
   *'A leader is best when people barely know he exists, when his work is done, his aim fulfilled, they will say: we did it ourselves.'*

2  On questions
   *'Learn from yesterday, live for today, hope for tomorrow. The important thing is not to stop questioning.'*

3  On learning
   *'Learning is not child's play; we cannot learn without pain.'*

4  On change
   *'People are always telling me that change is good. But all that means is that something you didn't want to happen has happened.'*

5  On social skills
   *'Conversation about the weather is the last refuge of the unimaginative.'*

Oscar Wilde (playwright); Meg Ryan (actress); Albert Einstein (scientist); Aristotle (philosopher); Lao Tzu (philosopher)

**HOT TIPS**

- If your humour isn't relevant to the topic of the presentation, don't use it
- Improve your presentation with a couple of quotations
- Remember: don't tell jokes; you may not be very funny!

1 Lao Tzu   2 Albert Einstein   3 Aristotle   4 Meg Ryan   5 Oscar Wilde

**Humour can work**

Once when Barbara Bush was asked to speak at the Wellesley College graduation ceremony, a large number of the all-female graduates-to-be felt that she was not the appropriate speaker since her accomplishments had been a result of her husband George Bush's presidency. However, in spite of the protests, the school kept Mrs Bush on the program. Immediately after being introduced, Mrs Bush said this: 'Someone in this audience may someday preside over the White House as the spouse* of the President and I wish him well.' Her comment was met with overwhelming applause and she quickly won over the audience.

*husband or wife

# Learning diary – starting presentations

### How to use your learning diary

This learning diary is designed to help you improve how you start presentations. Photocopy it and use it regularly so you can improve over the long term. Ideally you should:

1 Complete Part 1 and Part 2 before a presentation.

2 After the presentation, ask your audience for feedback. Get their opinions on the points which you identified in Part 2 as your improvement targets.

3 Write any comments from your audience in the feedback box.

4 Use this audience feedback to identify future improvement targets for your next presentation.

Finally, maintain this learning cycle until you can't find any more improvements to make.

### Part 1: What did I learn about starting presentations in this module?

11 **Feeling confident** ......................................................................................................

...................................................................................................................................

12 **The first three minutes** .............................................................................................

...................................................................................................................................

13 **Objectives or benefits?** .............................................................................................

...................................................................................................................................

14 **Starting with impact** ................................................................................................

...................................................................................................................................

15 **Using humour** ...........................................................................................................

...................................................................................................................................

### Part 2: Which three areas of the start will I try to improve?

Target for improvement 1: ..............................................................................................

Target for improvement 2: ..............................................................................................

Target for improvement 3: ..............................................................................................

### Part 3: Audience feedback about my opening

### Part 4: Which three areas of starting a presentation will I improve next?

1 ...............................................................................................................................

2 ...............................................................................................................................

3 ...............................................................................................................................

# Engaging international audiences

*'Business is not just doing deals; business is having great products, doing great engineering, and providing tremendous service to customers. Finally, business is a cobweb of **human** relationships.'* H Ross Perot

Time and time again professionals who are working internationally say that relationship building, creating Perot's cobweb, is the central success factor for international business. In fact, working life depends upon the relationships which we can create and cultivate with a wide range of individuals, from colleagues, managers, suppliers and customers through to coaches, mentors and external consultants.

International presenters also require relationship management skills – rapport-building, influencing, managing conflict – to engage and to connect to their international audiences effectively. In this module we will look at these skills and provide practical ideas on building relationships with audiences more quickly and more effectively.

# 16 Building rapport

Building rapport is an essential international competence. Worldwork's *International Profiler*[1], a psychometric tool for developing intercultural competence, defines individuals with this competence as people who:

— develop connections on a personal as well as a professional level

— are able to establish trust in different ways

— show warmth and attentiveness when building relationships

— choose behaviours that are comfortable for international partners

— build a sense of 'we'.

Let's look at how presenters can build this sense of 'we'.

## First contacts

When does a presentation begin?

- When an audience member first hears of the presentation event?
- When the audience begins to enter the room?
- When the presenter begins the presentation?

A presentation begins the moment an audience member hears about the event and starts planning to attend. At this point, impressions of the topic and of the presenter begin to form, along with expectations of the likely benefits and outcomes. If these impressions and expectations are positive, the presenter is already winning before a single word is spoken. So let's think about how presenters can achieve this.

### Tips for pre-presentation email and telephone contacts with your audience

- **Contact** key decision-makers to get a feel for their thinking on the topic.
- **Express** positive thoughts about meeting the individual participants.
- **Stress** concrete benefits to the individuals attending the presentation.

### Strategies for building rapport quickly with your audience before you begin

A presentation is a social moment providing important networking opportunities. Seize the opportunity to welcome individual audience members the moment they enter the room, to get to know them a little and to put them in the right mood to receive your message. Follow these tips to manage first contacts effectively:

1 **Welcome positively** Remember, it's not only what you say, it's how you say it. Blend friendly body language such as a smile, strong eye contact and committed handshake with a few positive words.

2 **Be curious – ask questions** An individual will feel welcomed if you ask polite questions about travel and accommodation, for example.

3 **Show knowledge** Show that you know something about them and their professional situation. Sometimes it pays to do a little research beforehand.

[1] www.worldwork.biz

4 **Build a bond by finding common points** Begin the process of connecting to people by signalling that you have points in common: people you may both know or something you have in common in your personal background.

Look at these sentences used by a presenter to build rapport with his audience before a presentation in India. Match them to the correct rapport-building strategy 1–4 above.

a  Maybe you know Peter Ronzoni? Peter and I worked together a lot last year.  ☐

b  Where are you staying?  ☐

c  Is this your first time in Delhi?  ☐

d  Did you fly in this morning?  ☐

e  So, you worked on the ESE project. I heard it went very well.  ☐

f  You're from Mumbai? Really? I visit Mumbai quite regularly.  ☐

g  I think that SAP is being implemented in your office right now, is that right?  ☐

h  It's really good to meet you.  ☐

- **Do** maximise body language: when meeting someone for the first time, be proactive and move towards them positively to show enthusiasm. Don't wait for others to approach you.
- **Don't** under-estimate the opportunity to shape positive expectations of your presentation by pre-presentation contacts
- **Do** continue all these person-oriented processes into the presentation itself. Treat the audience as a single person and talk to this person as if you were building a relationship for the longer term.

a 4   b 2   c 2   d 2   e 3   f 4   g 3   h 1

### Rapport-building styles

In order to manage relationships with different international audiences effectively, it's important to be aware that alternative rapport-building styles exist.

Communication experts have identified two important rapport-building styles: the reactive style and the proactive style.

### The reactive style

People with the reactive style prefer to be themselves, to react to circumstances and let things happen. They can come across to others as rather reserved and serious. Reactives don't like what they see as superficial and false politeness – asking lots of questions, smiling, being very warm and friendly. They prefer to be open and honest, even if this risks coming across as a little direct, even rude. Reactives like relationships to develop more naturally over time.

### The proactive style

People with the proactive style work hard to create an atmosphere of warm politeness, where people can communicate in an enthusiastic way to create a positive relationship quickly. This rapport-building style is characterised by the use of a lot of questions (to signal interest in people) and by an active style of listening which gives positive feedback to the speaker with phrases such as *Really?* or *That's interesting*. Conflict and negativity is to be avoided with the proactives who are happy to hide true feelings in favour of smiles and laughter to maintain a positive atmosphere.

Both presenter and audience can have each of these two styles:

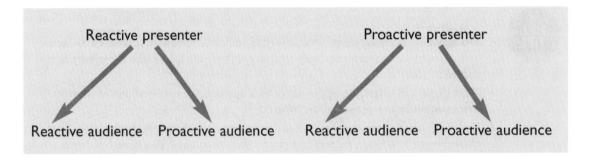

Presenters must be sensitive to their own individual style and the general style of their audience. Proactive presenters who smile and want to create a relaxed and friendly atmosphere may be understood by reactive-style audiences as a little superficial, just adapting behaviour to gain confidence; playing games and appearing friendly, when in fact there is another motive.

On the other hand, the proactive-style audience will find the reactive style presenter to be cold, inflexible, impolite, possibly over-direct and maybe even a little arrogant. Of course, these are generalisations but they are the kinds of feelings people often report about their international experience. Recognising and managing these people differences is a critical competence for international presenters.

**ASK YOURSELF**

What is your preferred rapport-building style – reactive or proactive?

How effectively can you build rapport with those who have an opposite style?

**HOT TIPS**

- Realise that relationship-building is critical to success in international business
- Maximise pre-presentation contacts to build rapport with audiences
- Analyse your own rapport-building style

# 17 Making things interesting

Some audiences demand more than information – they want to be entertained. Some speakers can communicate in ways which audiences find interesting and engaging with very little effort. But how exactly do they do it? What are their secrets? Well, as the saying goes: variety is the spice of life. Engaging and interesting speakers offer a great deal of variety in their communication style.

Look at these extracts from two presentations explaining the cancellation of a project to stakeholders. The first uses a narrower and neutral style based on short and simple statements. The second uses a more engaging style with far greater variety of sentence type.

**Version 1**

> ❝ So, to conclude, we have decided to scrap the project mainly because of financial and resource reasons which would have created difficulties for the organisation. I think this decision will save us around 140,000 each. We don't think we had any other option. Do you have any questions? ❞

**Version 2**

> ❝ Look, why did we decide to scrap the project? To be honest, we had other options. We could have simply postponed. We could have extended the deadlines. I said no. Two years ago we might have hesitated. Today we have to be more decisive. If we had hesitated, we would have lost more money, we would have committed more resources and we would have created many major difficulties for the organisation. So, come on, when you look at your next cost budget sitting in your office on a Friday afternoon, think of me a little, because I guess I saved each of you over 140,000. That is a massive saving for each of you this year. It's the biggest single saving you will make this year. When I mentioned the figure to my boss yesterday you should have seen her smile. So this decision was rational, logical and absolutely necessary, and I hope clear now to all of you as the key stakeholders. OK, thanks for listening to my sales pitch. I'm sure you have a few questions about this, as the project was very important to many of you. Jean? Peter? ❞

Version 2 is clearly much longer and requires more preparation, and more time to deliver, too. But the key point is that it engages the audience in the decision-making process.

### Strategies to develop interest and engagement

Here are some ideas to employ in your presentation.

**Using 'we'**    Presenters who use *we* can create a sense of solidarity with their audiences: *I think my presentation shows that we are making very good progress.*

**Integrating relevant, personal anecdotes**    Personal and amusing anecdotes can lighten and focus a presentation effectively:

> ❝I was asking my seven-year-old son the other day why he supported Manchester United. His answer was 'Quality. Quality matters to me.' And you know what, although I don't agree with him about Manchester United, I agree with him about quality. Quality does matter. ❞

**Simplifying**    *To be quite honest, we had no other option.*

**Creating a sense of urgency**    Using informal conversational expressions such as *Look ... , Listen ...* or *Come on* can create a mood of urgency and impact during a presentation.

**Making impacts tangible and personal**    The second version connects to the daily reality of the audience to touch and stimulate personally: *... when you look at your next cost budget sitting in your office on a Friday afternoon ...*

**Using strong words and facts**    Strong words and facts stand out more than neutral statements: *We have massive problems*, not ~~We have a lot of problems~~, or *It's the biggest single saving you will make this year*, not ~~You can save a lot of money.~~

**Asking rhetorical questions**    Rhetorical questions are hugely under-used by non-native speakers. Question–answer structures create a real dynamic for an audience: *Why did we decide to scrap the project? To be honest, we had other options.*

**Contrasting time frames**    Contrasting time frames also creates a logical momentum: *Two years ago we might have hesitated. Today we have to be more decisive.*

**Employing irony**    Humour is a higher-risk strategy, but when used effectively it can raise a smile and energise the moment: *Sorry if I bored you with that presentation.*

**Engaging people with the use of names**    Finally, don't under-estimate the power of using people's names: *I'm sure you have a few questions about this as the project was very important to many of you. Jean? Peter?*

Some may think it is unfair to call on people by name in the audience. But it certainly keeps people's attention if they believe they may be involved.

**TEST YOURSELF**

Match the two halves of these extracts from a presentation about quality management.

1  So why does this organisation need to improve quality?

2  Next time you're sitting there on a Friday afternoon having to write a customer proposal,

3  You may not agree with me about this.

4  I can say it in three words.

5  In the past it was possible to offer lower quality if the price was right.

a  Customers want quality.

b  think about adding 10% more quality to make sure the customer accepts it.

c  Tomorrow this won't be possible.

d  Basically, because our customers are demanding more and more of it.

e  John and Dave, I know you have very strong views. But let's take a bit of time today to talk through some alternatives to improving quality.

Before you check your answers, identify which strategy from page 49 each extract presents.

**ASK YOURSELF**

How can I make the presentation interesting for my audiences?

**HOT TIPS**

• Variety is the spice of life
• Think about rhetorical style when planning the presentation
• Create interesting messages to be more persuasive

1 d (asking rhetorical questions)    2 b (making impacts tangible and personal)
3 e (engaging people with the use of names)    4 a (simplifying)
5 c (contrasting time frames)

# 18 How to influence people

Influencing strategies and behaviours are situation-specific. For example, what persuades in one context may fail in another, depending on the power and authority you have. Presenting as a seller to a customer is very different to when a buyer is talking to a supplier. In fact, buyers can present requirements in a way which pressures suppliers to reduce prices and increase service level agreements. So, assess your power position and then consider the influencing strategies below.

## Influencing strategies

**Building trust**   People will only be influenced by those they trust. One essential factor is that audiences believe you have the right expertise.

 **ASK YOURSELF** Does your audience know enough about you to trust in your judgement, your experience and your skills?

**Employing logic**   At the end of the day, people are often convinced by good arguments and solid data.

 **ASK YOURSELF** Do you have the right data and are you able to get it across to others in a logical and articulate manner?

**Meeting needs**   People are more likely to be influenced if a presenter is offering something which meets their goals. In fact, this is often seen as the single biggest influencing factor. Interestingly, we may influence less by telling people what they need but more by asking people what they want, and then presenting solutions to satisfy this want.

 **ASK YOURSELF** How far as a presenter do you ask and answer the right questions?

**Stressing the relationship**   People are more open to influence from presenters they like, someone they have something in common with, someone they judge to be polite and approachable with a sense of humour.

How would your audiences judge your social skills?

**Creating personal impact**   Presenters create impact in a number of ways. Some go for a high-energy and more passionate approach to influencing; others go for a quieter, more reflective and analytical style.

What is your style and how far can you adapt to audiences which prefer a different one?

**Focusing assertively**   Audiences are likely to be influenced by presenters who communicate their ideas forcefully, clearly and persistently. But aggression is unlikely to influence. This is an important intercultural issue, as assertiveness and persistence in some contexts may be interpreted as aggression in others.

How far will audiences view you as assertive or aggressive?

**Being explicit**   Presenters who explain their reasoning openly and clearly will be seen by audiences as honest and committed to win–win outcomes. Presenters who fail to explain fully the thinking behind their ideas may be viewed as tactical, playing power games and attempting to manipulate their audience. It may take more time to be explicit, but the benefits are clear.

How far do your audiences believe you explain your thinking and reasoning sufficiently?

**Focusing on the future**   Presenters who provide a clear vision of the future with step-by-step guidance on how to reach that vision will be more engaging and influential. For some audiences, vision is best communicated with inspirational anecdotes or stories rather than facts and figures.

How far you do provide a clear and inspirational future vision for your audiences?

**Demonstrating self-confidence**   Presenters who come across as supremely self-confident can be influential without sophisticated arguments and solid data. However, there is a fine line between appearing self-confident and appearing arrogant.

Could an audience ever view you as arrogant?

**Transmitting optimism**   Negative presenters who focus on problems seldom inspire. Positive thinkers with energy and enthusiasm dedicated to finding creative solutions are more appealing to audiences.

How far do audiences see me as positive or negative?

**How to develop an influencing plan**
Presenters can use the strategies above to create an influencing plan for their presentations. There are two steps to follow:

**Step 1**   select which strategy to use according to the audience and context.

**Step 2**   note down what to say and do to achieve influence with each technique.

**TEST YOURSELF**

Read these notes that a presenter made for herself. Match them to the individual parts of the influencing strategy on pages 51–53.

1 *Let them know that they will lose competitive advantage in the future if they don't upgrade now. If they are still unsure, let them know that competitors have bought the product.* ......................

2 *Tell them about a recent independent report on new product. Really stress some of the cost-saving figures which were given.* ......................

3 *Arrive early and allow plenty of time for small talk before the presentation to get people in the right mood.* ......................

4 *Begin the presentation with some questions to the audience about current requirements in the organisation and then point out how the new product meets these requirements.* ......................

Now create an influencing strategy for your next presentation using the same two-step process.

**HOT TIPS**

• Analyse the power you have in the relationship before you plan how to influence
• Plan how to influence using the strategies in this module

1 Focusing on the future   2 Employing logic   3 Stressing the relationship   4 Meeting needs

# 19 Storytelling

Since the beginnings of humankind storytelling has taught, informed and entertained. Traditionally, oral stories were a means of transferring culture: bridging from the past to the present to make history memorable.

Today, leaders and presenters create memorable stories but to engage, to inform, to inspire, and to influence, to move audiences from a present situation to a future vision in a way which would be impossible with a simple explanation of facts and figures.

In this unit we will look at two story-telling techniques: the personal anecdote and the fantasy story.

## The personal anecdote

Personal anecdotes are the most frequently-used story-telling technique. Anecdotes have the advantage of making the presenter seem human. Personal stories can connect audience and speaker at an emotional level with listeners encouraged to experience reality through the eyes, ears and feelings of the storyteller.

Let's take a look at some different anecdote types which you can use to engage and to influence.

### 1   An insight into personal values
Telling a short story about yourself, for example how you faced a difficult choice, an embarrassing moment or how you achieved success unexpectedly, can be a perfect way to reveal personal values and establish a basis for others to know, respect and trust you.

### 2   A learning experience
Telling a story which shows how you gained insight into a current problem is a common device to promote acceptance of a solution which you are advocating. Sharing a learning experience, particularly if it is personal and even painful, is a powerful way to back up a solution you are promoting.

### 3   A moment of confusion
Telling a story about a misunderstanding you once experienced – either you misunderstood someone or they misunderstood you – can be an interesting way to ask an audience not to misunderstand you. The anecdote should promote open thinking to what might be rather unpleasant content in your presentation.

### 4   A tale of persistence
Telling a story about perseverance, of persistence in the face of hardship, of success against all odds, is a great way to raise spirits at difficult times and motivate people to continue believing with a 'Never say die' attitude. These stories tend to rely on anecdotes from famous historical or contemporary figures, but work better if they touch on an element of the presenter's own life story.

**Do it yourself**

Plan your own insight into personal values story using this structure:

- explain a past situation and a difficult choice you were facing
- tell the audience why the choice was difficult
- tell them what choice you made, and the results of that choice
- say what that decision-making process taught you about your personal values
- demonstrate how this learning process is relevant to the current working context.

## The fantasy story

For the more adventurous, there's always the possibility of being a modern-day Hans Christian Andersen and creating your own fairy story. Here's a four-step model to enable you to develop a truly memorable perspective on business problems through the use of fantasy story-telling.

### 1 Do it at the right time

Telling a story is a higher-risk presentation style. It requires performance skills and an audience ready and willing to participate in the game. If the audience is not ready, such a technique can leave you exposed and looking rather foolish. So, by all means plan to integrate a story into your presentation, but judge the mood of the audience on the day. If you don't feel you've created the necessary rapport to tell the story, play safe and drop it. If you do go for it, you may want to introduce an occasional touch of irony as you go through the story, just to avoid any feeling that you might be taking this story-telling business too seriously.

### 2 Create a scenario

You need a situation with a hero or heroine facing a monumental challenge. Remember, it's the eventual victory against huge odds which is the dynamic of a good story so we need passion and emotion built into the situation early. However, don't waste too much time in the set-up with boring detail or you'll lose the audience. Map out an archetypal framework quickly and sweep the audience towards the happy ending.

### 3 Narrate with passion

If the story has drama, you're going to need dramatic skills. Particularly important will be your voice, creating excitement with whispered descriptions and dramatic pauses, releasing the tension with increases in speed and volume, supported by dramatic gestures and movement. Remember, it is a high-risk style!

### 4 Build to a climax

Of course, the moral of the story always comes at the end. But don't labour it or you risk patronising your audience. Aim for a simple one-line statement to finish which allows the audience to get the point with maximum impact. Then move swiftly back to the business content of the presentation.

- Build up a bank of short and amusing personal anecdotes
- Rehearse telling these anecdotes
- Use fantasy stories if, and only if, you have the right performance skills

**The Echo Of Life**

A man and his son were walking in the forest. Suddenly the boy trips and, feeling a sharp pain, he screams, 'Ahhhhh!' Surprised, he hears a voice coming from the mountain, 'Ahhhhh!' Filled with curiosity, he shouts, 'Who are you?' but the only answer he receives is 'Who are you?' This makes him angry, so he shouts. 'You are a coward!' and the voice answers, 'You are a coward!'

He looks at his father asking, 'Dad, what is going on?' 'Son,' he replies, 'pay attention!' Then he shouts, 'I admire you!' The voice answers, 'I admire you!' The father shouts, 'You are wonderful!' and the voice answers, 'You are wonderful!'

The boy is surprised, but still can't understand what is going on. Then the father explains. 'People call this "echo", but truly it is life! Life always gives you back what you give out. Your life is not a coincidence, but a mirror of your own doings.'

http://www.learntofeelgood.com/stories.html

Find more stories at http://www.timsheppard.co.uk/story/stories/pentamerone.html.

# 20  Let's get interactive

Presentations exist to engage audiences, yet so many presenters use *PowerPoint* to create silent and passive audiences staring at the projected information. Let's look at some ideas to help interaction.

## Planning interactivity

Presenters face three big questions when planning interactive audience activities:

**When** – fun activities are very useful when you want to build a positive climate for a presentation and to introduce key ideas early in a non-threatening way. Importantly, activities can deflect attention from the speaker and so reduce stress.

**Who** – the presenter has to decide on numbers for the activity. Should the activity focus on one individual (a volunteer in front of the audience), pair work (ask your partner) or involve smaller sub-groups or the whole audience?

**What** – presenters have to consider two issues:

- the style of the task, for example draw something, define something, solve a problem, compete over something.
- how to exploit the results of the group work. Is it displayed and reviewed? Is it summarised in written or verbal form or is it just a quick request for feedback from presenter to audience?

Remember, if you take too much time on the briefing and debriefing, you risk losing all the momentum of the activity itself.

## Some activities to try in your presentations

### Who am I?

This is a fun activity with smaller audiences. Label each corner of the room as an animal, e.g. tiger, eagle, shark and squirrel. Then ask audience members to go to the corner which best describes their personality. This could form a simple get-to-know exercise with people forming groups and introducing themselves. It can be extended to the theme of the presentation. For example, in a presentation on leadership, you could link the qualities of the various animals to qualities of leadership. Alternatively, you could ask the group members to take up a position defined by how their customers and suppliers see them. This is a very good way to start a discussion on business stakeholder relationships. Use it as a great ice-breaker or mid-talk energiser.

### What do you think?

For many people in business, networking at presentations is as important as the talk itself. Encouraging exchanges between audience members can prove very popular. Here are some simple tasks to be done in pairs or threes to support networking:

A definition-style task: *Give three words you associate with customer service!*

A hypothetical task: *What would you do if … ?*

An experience survey: *Have you ever … ?*

A direct question: *What is the best way to … ?*

You can use these tasks as simple ice-breakers or as activities to find out the opinion of audience members on a key topic before you begin speaking. A more anonymous way to get thoughts from an audience is to ask them to write down opinions onto cards. These cards are then passed around the room with audience members adding more opinions. After a few minutes of fun, the presenter says stop and asks people to read out what is written on the cards in their hands. Try it – it works!

### Group dynamics

I once gave a presentation on effective international teamwork to over sixty people. After ten minutes of speaking, I split people into groups and asked them to come up with rules that their international team should follow over the next twelve months. This activity can be very effective with very large groups, allowing a real exchange of ideas. Groups could include a slogan, a pledge, a logo or even a small dramatised role play illustrating a core principle.

### And the winner is ...

Don't under-estimate the energy which a little competition can create. Short quizzes, particularly at the end, can produce a strong feel-good factor to finish off with. Make sure you have fun prizes not only for the winner but for second and third places!

### Five turn-offs for audiences

1 Tasks which are too difficult

2 Tasks which are irrelevant

3 Tasks which are too childish

4 Tasks which are focused too closely on sensitive topics

5 Tasks which require too much time for the briefing and debriefing

**HOT TIPS**

- Don't rely on simply telling your audience things – involve them
- Plan tasks with the right when, who and what
- Use ideas which you have seen tried and tested by other presenters

# Learning diary – engaging international audiences

### How to use your learning diary

This learning diary is designed to help you engage international audiences. Photocopy it and use it regularly so you can improve over the long term. Ideally you should:

1 Complete Part 1 and Part 2 before a presentation.

2 After the presentation, ask your audience for feedback. Get their opinions on the points which you identified in Part 2 as your improvement targets.

3 Write any comments from your audience in the feedback box.

4 Use this audience feedback to identify future improvement targets for your next presentation.

Finally, maintain this learning cycle until you can't find any more improvements to make.

### Part 1: What did I learn about engaging international audiences in this module?

16 **Building rapport** ...........................................................................................................

.............................................................................................................................................

17 **Making things interesting** ..........................................................................................

.............................................................................................................................................

18 **How to influence people** .............................................................................................

.............................................................................................................................................

19 **Storytelling** ...................................................................................................................

.............................................................................................................................................

20 **Let's get interactive** .....................................................................................................

.............................................................................................................................................

### Part 2: Which three areas of engaging audiences will I try to improve?

Target for improvement 1: ...........................................................................................

Target for improvement 2: ...........................................................................................

Target for improvement 3: ...........................................................................................

### Part 3: Audience feedback about my audience engagement

### Part 4: Which three areas of my audience engagement will I improve next?

1 ...........................................................................................................................................

2 ...........................................................................................................................................

3 ...........................................................................................................................................

# Developing a range of styles

*'Among giants be a dwarf; among dwarfs be a giant, but among equals aim to be an equal.'* Stanislaw Jilec

Your success as a presenter depends in part on your ability to deliver the information with the right communication style. Being informal, friendly and interactive may be highly successful with some audiences but fail with others who believe professional presenters should offer direct, weighty and serious analysis without a smile. It's vital to develop an awareness of differing expectations of 'good' presentation style in order to get your message across effectively to a range of audiences.

In this module we will look at the features of four important presentation styles: the powerful, the balancing, the questioning and the personal. It is important to state that this analysis of different styles is not completely objective. Individuals will view the communication style of a presenter quite differently, based upon their own preferences. However, reflecting on these styles will, in the final unit, enable you to develop your own style so that you can adapt to different situations.

21  **The powerful style**

22  **The balancing style**

23  **The questioning style**

24  **The personal style**

25  **Getting the style right**

# 21 The powerful style

Professionals who see themselves as highly analytical and very results-focused often use the powerful style.

## The powerful style in action

Many audiences will see a presenter who uses the powerful style as strong and competent. Others may interpret the same style as aggressive, even arrogant.

Look at this extract from a presentation by an oil executive about falling petroleum prices to see the powerful style in action.

> ❛Look, we must take action immediately and reduce our prices. There's absolutely no option here. Peter, I know you have a different opinion but I think you're wrong. I think it would be totally ridiculous and wrong to wait while our competitors reduce their prices and start stealing our customers. So, I've prepared an action plan which will serve as a structure for my presentation. There are just two points, in fact: how much to reduce and for which channels. As I said, it's obvious from the data we have that the market is not going to change in the short term, so we have to react in the only way possible. So, let me move to the first point: the amount by which we need to reduce our prices. ❜

**TEST YOURSELF**

Read through these features of the powerful style. Then re-read the presentation extract above and find example phrases and sentences for each feature.

### Conviction

Presenters who use the powerful style tend to use forceful language such as *must have to*, *impossible* or *can't* to put their messages across. They may stress their own knowledge of the subject or introduce facts from other authorities to make it difficult to disagree with them. In general, strong statements are made with very few questions asked.

..................................................................................................................................

### Personal confrontation

Presenters may disagree directly with other viewpoints using phrases such as *You're wrong* or *That's not true*.

..................................................................................................................................

### Control

There is not very much negotiation of the presentation process. Powerful presenters tend to decide the best way to structure things and prefer to announce the organisation of the presentation in the introduction without any offer to re-sequence the points in line with audience preferences or needs.

..................................................................................................................................

**Pressure**

Pressure is created – *Time is short! Budgets cannot be exceeded! Remember I'm the boss* – to persuade others.

........................................................................................................................................

**The non-verbal factor**

People can come across as powerful and authoritative if they have a loud and emphatic voice which is backed up with stiffness in body language and seriousness in facial expression.

**Analysing your own communication style**

- How much do you like the style of the extract?
- How many features of the powerful style do you think you use?
- How many features of the powerful style could you use if you wanted?
- How many of your international audiences see you as a powerful-style speaker?
- In which of your work situations would presenting in this style be:
  a) productive?
  b) counter-productive?

**HOT TIPS**

- Always remember to see yourself through your audience's eyes
- Develop your own powerful style for audiences which expect this
- Implement your own powerful style at the right time in the right place

**Suggested answers**

Conviction: *There's absolutely no option here | I think it would be totally ridiculous and wrong | As I said, it's obvious | we have to react in the only way possible*
Personal confrontation: *Peter, … I think you're wrong*
Control: *So, I've prepared an action plan*
Pressure: *Look, we must take action immediately | wrong to wait while our competitors … start stealing our customers.*

63

# 22 The balancing style

In many ways the balancing style stands as an opposite to the powerful style.

## The balancing style in action

Many audiences will see a presenter who uses the balancing style as open and ready to negotiate at all times. Others may interpret the same style as weak and indecisive.

Look at this extract from a presentation by another oil executive about falling petroleum prices, this time presented in the balancing style.

> ❛OK, it may be necessary to take action quite quickly and think about reducing our prices a little. Peter, I fully understand your point of view but I have the feeling that we are under a little pressure because the actions of our competitors have started to have an impact on our customer base. If it's OK with everybody here, I'd like to take a look at an action plan which I've drawn up as a starting point for discussion of next steps. I've identified two points which we have enough time to look at in detail: a proposed amount of reduction and then a focus on channels. You probably have other points to add to this, of course. I think we could move forward in a number of ways although I'm sure you also have opinions about options. But how shall we proceed? Shall I give a short input or would you prefer to do this in another way? ❜

**TEST YOURSELF**

Read through these features of the balancing style. Then re-read the presentation extract above and find example phrases and sentences for each feature.

**Future possibilities**
Presenters who use the balancing style try to come across as open to their audience by stressing future possibilities and avoiding strong statements of certainty. In other words, they try to avoid the impression that they have a definitive or final answer, and will use words like *may, might* or *probably*, and other words or phrases which they believe indicate openness.

...........................................................................................................................

**Conflict avoidance**
For the balancing style, indirectness is a way to avoid confrontation so that people don't disagree directly. Instead, the positive in what others say is usually acknowledged, even when disagreeing, with phrases such as *You may be right, but* ... or *I see what you're saying, but* ... . Opinions may be softened so that they sound less absolute, for example *It's a little difficult* or *It's not so easy* rather than *It's impossible*.

...........................................................................................................................

### Involvement in process

For the balancing style it is important to negotiate the presentation and discussion process itself in order not to be seen as controlling and directive. Presenters will ask questions from time to time to check that the audience is happy with proceedings – *Is this structure fine for you?* – and are always open to negotiate a new way, for example *Shall we do this another way?*

### Time-relaxed

Balancing presenters try not to pressurise the audience, preferring a calm working environment where everyone can be heard and a full analysis can be carried out. They may try to stress that there is enough time to think further before taking a decision, and that it is important to carry out a full analysis, for example *I don't think we need to rush things or I think it's important to consider all views.*

### The non-verbal factor

People can come across as balancing if they moderate their voice and body language to seem facilitating and open. They may not speak so quickly and will maintain good eye contact with people to signal respect.

### Analysing your own communication style

- How much do you like the style of the extract?
- How many features of the balancing style do you think you use?
- How many features of the balancing style could you use if you wanted?
- How many of your international audiences see you as a balancing-style speaker?
- In which of your work situations would presenting in this style be:
  a) productive?
  b) counter-productive?

**HOT TIPS**

- Always remember to see yourself through your audience's eyes
- Develop your own balancing style for audiences which expect this
- Implement your own balancing style at the right time in the right place

**Suggested answers**
Future possibilities: *OK, it may be necessary | I think we could move forward in a number of ways*
Conflict avoidance: *think about reducing our prices a little | Peter, I fully understand your point of view | we are under a little pressure*
Involvement in process: *If it's OK with everybody here | But how shall we proceed? Shall I give a short input or would you prefer to do this in another way?*
Time-relaxed: *which we have enough time to look at in detail*

# 23 The questioning style

It may seem strange to use the term questioning style for a presenter, but questions can be used as a core communication strategy to achieve very specific outcomes.

## The questioning style in action

Many audiences will see a presenter who uses the questioning style as a dynamic and interactive speaker, interested in listening to others' opinions in order to develop customised solutions. Others will interpret the same style as demonstrating a lack of expertise, a failure to take responsibility for transmitting expert information from presenter to audience in as short a time as possible.

Look at this extract from a presentation about new solutions by a sales manager from a software company to a key account customer.

**Presenter:** Right, today I'd like to introduce two new solutions which I believe might be interesting for your organisation. To start, if I may, I just want to ask a couple of questions. Firstly, how much pressure are you under to reduce costs?

**Audience member:** A lot. You know we have the new business model to implement.

**Presenter:** Right. But you need software with new functionalities, especially in the management of financial data. Yes?

**Audience member:** Absolutely.

**Presenter:** And these are the two big questions and pressures facing you: you have to cut costs and yet you need to invest in new software functionality. This is pretty much the same for all our clients, so we started to think, 'Is there anything we can do to offer more for less?' And we started looking. What if we simplified the program? Didn't work because we lost functionality. How far could we add new functionality cheaply? This proved to be impossible. So we had a big problem. And what did we do? Well, we eventually came up with a big answer, by which I mean a very effective solution. In fact, we've found we can rework our existing program and generate new and compatible functionality and reduce costs by lowering service requirements. How does that sound?

**Audience member:** It sounds good. Tell me more!

## Asking real questions

Presenters ask audiences questions for three reasons:

1 Questions allow presenters to get information from the audience which can be used to introduce and explain the logic of the presentation. Typical strategies are to ask the audience questions to identify gaps in knowledge, for example *What do our customers want from us today?* or to investigate problems and solutions, for example *What do you think caused the problem?* or *What do you think we need to do?* Answers then form the logic of the presentation content, for example *So, that's what I want to look at today. What do our customers need and how can we meet that need?*

2 Questions allow presenters to clarify things – the real reason for a problem, the current status of a project, the success of failure of an initiative – in order to tailor input more correctly to the audience knowledge level and needs.

3 Questions allow audiences to get involved, to participate, to give and exchange opinions. This can have a very positive effect on the dynamic of a presentation.

## Asking rhetorical questions

Rhetorical questions are not real questions. The presenter who asks a rhetorical question already knows the answer to the question. Presenters can exploit rhetorical questions in two main ways:

1 Presenters can bridge dynamically from the problem to their solution:

Problem:     *This is the problem.*

Challenge:   *And how do we solve it?*

Proposal:    *Well, our solution is to …*

2 Presenters can vary the flow of information to enhance the impact of their message and the engagement of the audience when discussing key business concepts such as costing and timing.

Timing:       *How soon do we need this? In my opinion, …*

Costing:      *How much will it cost? Well, according to our calculations …*

Forecasting:  *What will happen if we do this? I think …*

Reasoning:    *Why should we do this? The reason is …*

Allocating:   *Who is going to do this? After some thought, we've decided to …*

Meaning:      *What does this mean to us? I believe …*

**TEST YOURSELF**

Re-read the presentation extract on page 66 and find examples of the two types of question.

---

**Suggested answers**

Real questions: *Firstly, how much pressure are you under to reduce costs?* | *But you need software with new functionalities, especially in the management of financial data. Yes?* | *How does that sound?*

Rhetorical questions: *Is there anything we can do to offer more for less?* | *What if we simplified the program?* | *How far could we add new functionality cheaply?* | *And what did we do?*

**The non-verbal factor**

People can support their questioning role in a number of ways. Walking among a larger audience can support the impression of enquiry. Additionally, visually recording answers from the audience in some way, for example on a flip chart, is important. If ideas are not recorded, there is a danger the audience simply sees the questioning strategy as tactical and unreal.

**Analysing your own communication style**

- How much do you like the style of the extract?
- How many features of the questioning style do you think you use?
- How many features of the questioning style could you use if you wanted?
- How many of your international audiences see you as a questioning-style speaker?
- In which of your work situations would presenting in this style be:
  a) productive?
  b) counter-productive?

**HOT TIPS**

- Always remember to see yourself through your audience's eyes
- Develop a set of questions which you feel happy using when presenting
- Implement your own questioning style at the right time in the right place

# 24 The personal style

Business people are often very task or information oriented. However, communication always has a people side and presenters who employ the personal style manage this relationship dimension as well as the information dimension.

## The personal style in action

Many audiences will see a presenter who uses the personal style as warm and friendly, nice to be around, a likeable personality they enjoy being with. Others may interpret the same style as superficial, pretending to be friendly whilst keeping another agenda in the background, being too informal when business should be serious.

Look at this extract from a presentation by a human resources manager about developing people effectively to middle management.

> ❜So, let's turn to the issue of the new high potential development programme to be launched next year. Like you, I'm quite excited, to be honest, because I think that what we have here is going to be great for our young high-fliers. I'm confident that we will see very positive results within six months. Now, we've talked about this a lot in the past and so I know that we see things very much in the same way. Basically, we all want to support these young talents more, as they really do represent the future of the company. Peter, I know you feel very strongly about this issue and that was why I involved you from a very early phase in the project to develop a programme, and your contribution has been fantastic and absolutely critical to the process. So, with the excitement mounting, let's see if I can remember what I've written on these slides and give you an overview of the programme. ❜

**TEST YOURSELF**

Read through these features of the personal style. Then re-read the presentation extract above and find example phrases and sentences for each feature.

### Focus on positive results

Presenters with the personal style like to stress the positive at every opportunity. They will frequently use positive words like *good, great, interesting, useful* to express positive ideas, and praise people in order to generate an atmosphere where everyone feels good.

...................................................................................................................................

### Identify points in common

Presenters highlight things that they have in common with their audience. They share a similar perspective or experience; they have a similar objective; they want the same outcome.

...................................................................................................................................

### Work with feelings

The personal style involves feelings: both acknowledging the feelings of others –
*I know you feel very strongly about this* – and revealing your own feelings in an
open and honest way, for example *My own feelings about this, to be perfectly honest,
are quite mixed.*

### Build rapport with humour

Humour is very important to release and share positive energy. Humour can often
be ironic and self-directed, for example *Thank you for coming today. As it's Friday
afternoon I'll make sure we finish before five o'clock as I'm sure you're keen to get
home this evening rather listen to me for too long*, in order to promote modesty and
equality as core values.

### The non-verbal factor

Presenters support their personal style in a number of ways. They tend to speak
with a moderate volume and intonation which is comfortable for others. They will
also like positive eye contact and will tend to smile a lot.

### Analysing your own communication style

- How much do you like the style of the extract?
- How many features of the personal style do you think you use?
- How many features of the personal style could you use if you wanted?
- How many of your international audiences see you as a personal-style speaker?
- In which of your work situations would presenting in this style be:
  a) productive?
  b) counter-productive?

**HOT TIPS**

- Using 'we' rather than 'I' can build a personal connection with audiences
- Always remember to see yourself through your audience's eyes
- Develop your own personal style which is comfortable for both you and your
  international audiences

# 25 Getting the style right

There are three main steps to using the right presentation style:

**Step 1** is raising awareness of different styles

**Step 2** is increasing our ability to use a wider range of styles

**Step 3** is selecting the right style for the right context

To review, let's test your new awareness of presentation styles.

**TEST YOURSELF**

1 Match these styles to the extracts below.

Powerful ...... Balancing ...... Questioning ...... Personal ......

**Extract 1** ❝The main issue I want to look at today is how to improve safety on site. And there are a couple of questions which come to mind immediately: what is the current level of safety on site? [1].............. And also, what level of safety do we really want to achieve? And how much will it cost? Good questions but not so easy to find good answers. So what's the best way to find an answer? Well, I thought it would be useful to start by looking at the results of an internal audit and then move on to the future with a quick overview of some benchmarking studies. Is that OK with everyone? ❞

**Extract 2** ❝Right, to start this project off, I'd like to give a short introduction to myself. I know that may be possibly the most boring way to start the day but at least it will be out of the way. Well, I guess, like everybody here I've been with the company for over ten years. [2].............. The work is very interesting, the colleagues are great, most of them anyway, and I feel that I am developing here year on year. About the project we are about to start, I think ... ❞

**Extract 3** ❝The results from the last quarter are excellent. But we cannot be complacent. I don't agree with John when he says that we can downscale investment. [3].............. We have to capitalise on our advantage and attack the competition from a position of strength. I want to show you an action plan which explains how to capitalise and how to do it quickly ... ❞

**Extract 4** ❝Right, shall we move onto the next issue, the way to increase quality in production? I'm sure there are a number of ways to tackle this problem and there are some differences of opinion. John, I know you favour some form of certification, which I don't think is exactly the right way forward. [4].............. However, let's discuss further after my presentation. Of course, we should try to take a decision today, but we may need some time to reach a consensus ... ❞

2 Now complete the extracts with these phrases.
 a *That would be simply crazy and really not an option.*
 b *I think it might be a little expensive.*
 c *And to be perfectly honest, I like working here.*
 d *Do we really know the current status?*

### How flexible are you? Developing a range of styles

In order for you to develop more flexibility in your communication style, follow this learning plan.

1 **Develop more self-awareness**
   Record a segment of your next presentation with a camcorder. Look at your style of presenting and try to identify which of the four styles you seem to prefer. You may see elements of all four styles, but one will be more dominant.

2 **Plan using a range of styles**
   Write a short introduction to your next presentation using each of the four different styles you have studied.

3 **Experiment with new styles of behaviour**
   Record yourself presenting each of the four introductions with a camcorder. Analyse your performance using the following questions. In addition to this self-evaluation, it is vital that you get feedback from another person, as someone else's view of you may be very different from your own.

   Which style looks and sounds most natural for you?

   Which style looks and sounds most unnatural for you?

   Which aspects of your presentation style should you develop first?

Having developed sensitivity, the challenge remains to develop a greater range of presentation styles and then use the right style for the right context. The selection of style will be dependent on a number of factors, including national and corporate culture: for example, the power relationship you have with your audience (are you presenting to the board or to colleagues?), and on whether the audience is internal or external. There is no simple formula for success. Every presenter has to take a decision based on an analysis of the specific situation.

**HOT TIPS**

- Work to your strengths as a presenter and minimise any weaknesses
- Rehearse alternative communication styles in private
- Experiment carefully with new communication styles in real business contexts

1 Extract 1: Questioning   Extract 2: Personal   Extract 3: Powerful   Extract 4: Balancing
2 1 d   2 c   3 a   4 b

# Learning diary – developing a range of styles

### How to use your learning diary

This learning diary is designed to help you improve your range of communication styles for presenting. Photocopy it and use it regularly so you can improve over the long term. Ideally you should:

1 Complete Part 1 and Part 2 before a presentation.

2 After the presentation, ask your audience for feedback. Get their opinions on the points which you identified in Part 2 as your improvement targets.

3 Write any comments from your audience in the feedback box.

4 Use this audience feedback to identify future improvement targets for your next presentation.

Finally, maintain this learning cycle until you can't find any more improvements to make.

### Part 1: What did I learn about communication styles in this module?

21 **The powerful style** ...................................................................................................
...................................................................................................................................

22 **The balancing style** ..................................................................................................
...................................................................................................................................

23 **The questioning style** ...............................................................................................
...................................................................................................................................

24 **The personal style** ....................................................................................................
...................................................................................................................................

25 **Getting the style right** .............................................................................................
...................................................................................................................................

### Part 2: Which three areas of my communication style will I try to improve?

Target for improvement 1: ...........................................................................................

Target for improvement 2: ...........................................................................................

Target for improvement 3: ...........................................................................................

### Part 3: Audience feedback about my communication style

### Part 4: Which three areas of my communication style will I improve next?

1 ...........................................................................................................................

2 ...........................................................................................................................

3 ...........................................................................................................................

# It's not only words – non-verbal communication

*'Don't look at me in that tone of voice!'* David Farber

Albert Mehrabian is frequently quoted during discussions of non-verbal communication. His research in the 1950s revealed the importance of body language and voice when presenting. He judged that the total impact of a message is about 7% verbal (words only), 38% vocal (including tone of voice, inflection, and other sounds) and 55% non-verbal.

Although you may argue about the percentages, there is little doubt that effective presenters need to manage aspects of voice and body language effectively in order to get their message across.

Let's look at some ideas to improve your non-verbal communication.

26 **Using your voice effectively**

27 **Body language**

28 **Practice makes perfect**

29 **Goodbye to stress**

30 **Managing the physical environment**

# 26 Using your voice effectively

Ask yourself this question before you start your next presentation – *Do I have an interesting voice?* If you've answered *No, Not really* or *I don't know*, then this is an important unit for you.

## Critical success factors

Here are some ideas to improve the way you speak for presentations. There are five areas to consider.

### Volume

A common fault of presenters is not speaking loudly enough. Two tips: firstly, always check with people at the back of the room that they can hear you; secondly, continue talking at the right volume for these people. If you're using a microphone, don't have it too close to your mouth. Experiment with different distances before the presentation.

### Tempo

#### Tips for fast speakers

If you're a fast speaker, then you will probably have to slow down a little. Remember, fast speakers can be seen by some as energetic and dynamic, and by others as rather individualistic, aggressive and arrogant.

Relax and use more pauses between words and sentences. Practise speaking more slowly by speaking aloud paragraphs of text more and more slowly.

#### Tips for slow speakers

Slow speakers can be seen by some as analytical and prepared, and by others as uncreative and boring.

Think less analytically and become more tolerant of using the wrong word or making a grammatical mistake. Practise speaking faster by saying aloud paragraphs of text at increasing speeds.

In many ways, the secret is to ensure variety of tempo: faster in explanations and slower when making the really key points. And don't forget to control any stress you are feeling, as it causes most presenters to speed up a lot!

### Tone

The tone of your voice – whether you sound interested, bored, angry, nervous – has an enormous emotional impact on the listener. Again, there is no perfect model. Enthusiastic speakers will energise some audiences, but irritate others who may see this speaking style as unprofessional and self-promoting. A more serious voice with a flatter intonation will communicate expertise to some, but might send others to sleep.

Cultural differences add to this complexity. In the end, you should aim for a tone of voice which expresses professional expertise, personal warmth and a positive outlook: which could mean either injecting or reducing energy, according to your natural style. Ask people who know you well for their assessment of your voice and how you might communicate to a range of different audiences.

### Chunking

We develop impact when presenting by cutting sentences into chunks of meaning which we then emphasise with stress and pausing.

Try reading aloud this presentation extract to see how chunking enhances a message. Pause slightly at the end of each line and stress the words or parts of words in **bold** text.

There are **two big issues**

which we **must** talk about **today**.

**Firstly,**

there is the issue of **pro**duct range

and how **new** and **fierce** competition

presents a **real threat**.

**Secondly,**

we should look at **marketing,**

and where we've suc**ceed**ed

and **failed**

in the last two years

so we can build a really strong **action** plan

to support us in the **short**

**and**

in the **long** term.

**ASK YOURSELF**
How far do I speak with a similar rhythm when I present?

**Articulation**

Articulating words effectively makes you easy to understand. Be precise and controlled in your pronunciation.

**How to develop your voice**

**Step 1**   Listen to a recording of your own voice and evaluate yourself using the scales below. (10 is high, 1 is low)

Volume          10 – 9 – 8 – 7 – 6 – 5 – 4 – 3 – 2 – 1

Notes: ...............................................

Tempo           10 – 9 – 8 – 7 – 6 – 5 – 4 – 3 – 2 – 1

Notes: ...............................................

Tone            10 – 9 – 8 – 7 – 6 – 5 – 4 – 3 – 2 – 1

Notes: ...............................................

Chunking        10 – 9 – 8 – 7 – 6 – 5 – 4 – 3 – 2 – 1

Notes: ...............................................

Articulation    10 – 9 – 8 – 7 – 6 – 5 – 4 – 3 – 2 – 1

Notes: ...............................................

**Step 2**   Ask other people to rate your voice using the same scale.

**Step 3**   Develop an action plan based on these two ratings.

**HOT TIPS**

- Relax and breathe calmly in order to be able to speak effectively
- Drink plenty of water before and during a presentation to hydrate the vocal chords
- Experiment with different volumes, tempos and tones when you rehearse your presentation – this will give you more confidence to control your voice

# 27 Body language

What should I do with my hands? What's the best way to stand? Should I move or stay still? Presenters can become very self-conscious when standing in front of an audience, and they're right to be concerned. Poorly-managed self-presentation with awkward body language can make you appear unprofessional, greatly reducing the impact of your message. Let's look at some ways to improve your body language.

## Improving your body language

### Look at me when I'm talking to you
In many cultures it's important to maintain eye contact with your audience if you want to come across as confident, positive and truthful. However, many non-native speakers tend to lose eye contact too often for very obvious reasons:

— they look up and away from the audience when trying to recall English vocabulary; this is a typical eye movement when accessing memory

— they spend a lot of time looking at their slides and not at the audience so that they can see the English vocabulary they need to explain their point.

### Tips for effective eye contact
• Scan the audience, taking time to establish eye contact with specific individuals for around fifteen seconds, and then move on to the next person. This way individual members of the audience feel you are talking to and not at them.

• Avoid turning your back on the audience when presenting slide information. My advice is TTT, touch – turn – talk:

**Touch**   move a hand in the direction of the slide to indicate important information

**Turn**   turn your head to look directly at the audience

**Talk**   talk about the information.

### Give me a smile
Facial expressions support what we say. Determination, confidence, openness, friendliness are all communicated by facial expressions. Probably the single most underused expression is the smile. As we say, a smile never hurts!

### Don't point at me
Some body language experts recommend specific movements and gestures when presenting. They will argue that confident speakers don't keep their arms behind their backs or straight across the front of the body below the waist.

It is suggested that you keep hands and arms up around waist height; sometimes together, sometimes with one hand moving out to illustrate a point, like weather presenters on TV. It is also recommended that you use fingers in a specific way when describing points with numbers; thumb for point one; thumb and index finger for point two with the back of the hand facing the audience.

**Tips for using gestures**

- **Do** record yourself with a camcorder giving a presentation and note down effective and ineffective gestures.
- **Do** try to time gestures with the rhythm of your speech. All effective presenters synchronise the physical and the verbal.
- **Don't** use gestures which are unnatural for you. It will show!
- **Don't** point. It's rude.

**Stand and deliver**

Confident speakers have a powerful stance: they stand tall, with legs about shoulder width apart with weight evenly distributed. They control the space between themselves and the audience positively, sometimes approaching the audience, sometimes moving to examine the projected slide. Walking around is vital to animate a presentation, to create a dynamic movement which the audience has to track. But don't overdo it – too much movement can irritate as well as impress.

**How to improve body language**

**Step 1**    Watch a video recording of one of your presentations and evaluate yourself using the scales below (10 is high, 1 is low)

| Eye contact | 10 – 9 – 8 – 7 – 6 – 5 – 4 – 3 – 2 – 1 |
| | Notes: ............................................... |
| Facial expression | 10 – 9 – 8 – 7 – 6 – 5 – 4 – 3 – 2 – 1 |
| | Notes: ............................................... |
| Gesture | 10 – 9 – 8 – 7 – 6 – 5 – 4 – 3 – 2 – 1 |
| | Notes: ............................................... |
| Stance | 10 – 9 – 8 – 7 – 6 – 5 – 4 – 3 – 2 – 1 |
| | Notes: ............................................... |

**Step 2**    Ask others to rate your body language using the same scale.

**Step 3**    Develop an action plan based on these two ratings.

**Consider culture**

Be sensitive to the fact that all aspects of body language may vary enormously from culture to culture. Research your audience to find out the correct forms of eye contact, facial expression, gesture and stance/movement which may be expected. However, beware stereotyping, keep an open mind and adapt to the specific people who you are presenting to.

**HOT TIPS**

- Be yourself – if you are unnatural, people will sense it
- Be confident and relaxed – think positively and smile
- Get feedback in order to develop yourself

# 28 Practice makes perfect

So, that was the theory about voice and body language. Now let's turn to a little bit of fun practice which will enable you to explore your own abilities. Find a quiet room. Lock the door, stand in front of a mirror and allow your performance potential to shine during the following three exercises.

### Exercise 1

Let's practise chunking. Divide these presentation extracts into chunks of meaning by marking the main stresses and pauses. Then practise saying them with maximum impact. The objective is not to find the right answer – in fact, there are many possible answers – but more to practise using your voice differently and more effectively. If possible, do the exercise with a colleague and compare answers.

### Extract 1

‘ Are there any questions on that? Right, then the third point and the most important point for today is the issue of project staffing. As you know we will need three maybe even four people to go out to North America in January. And to be honest I'm not sure that we've got three or four people who are ready for the task. This represents a major challenge to the project and we need to find a solution today. ’

### Extract 2

‘ Let's look at our promotion options in more detail. Firstly we can just advertise the products in the national press. But this is expensive and very untargeted. The second option is to advertise again but in specialist trade magazines. This is cost-effective and reaches the target client. Thirdly and finally we could promote the products with a special brochure to our main customers. Although this is the most expensive I think it will produce by far the best return. ’

### Exercise 2

Now think of effective gestures and movements to accompany the extracts. Then say them again with these gestures and movements. Do it in front of a mirror so you can see how you would look to an audience.

**Exercise 3**

Now follow this four-step practice template with the introduction to your next presentation.

1 Script the opening three minutes.

2 Underline the stresses and mark any pauses on the text.

3 Plan gestures and movement to create maximum impact and then note down your ideas on the text.

4 Practise in front of the mirror until it feels natural.

**A final note on effective non-verbal communication**

Body language from an audience will tell you how effective you are at delivering an animating and engaging presentation. Hopefully, you won't see too many people:

… checking email

… twiddling thumbs

… drawing pictures

… drumming fingers

… flipping through your handout all the time

… whispering to other audience members

… with arms folded hoping for the end

… snoring but happy!

**HOT TIPS**

• Remember, how you speak and how you move affects the impact of your message

• Be prepared to experiment with voice and body language to communicate more effectively

• Be patient! Changing how you speak and move will feel unnatural at first

# 29 Goodbye to stress

Let's start with a simple statement of fact. Presentations are not stressful. Only presenters make presentations stressful. Positive thinking can make stress a thing of the past and transform presentations into a fun experience. So let's get rid of negative thinking and re-invent how we experience presentations.

### Get excited

What we sometimes call stress is actually better called excitement. It's a natural and very positive reaction by the body to produce adrenalin when faced with a challenge in order to sharpen the senses. If you aren't feeling excited, you aren't prepared, so recognise the feeling and be grateful for it. Your body is preparing you physically and mentally to perform well.

### Get real

There is a simple technique to really stress yourself the next time you present. All you have to do is decide that the quality of your presentation must be 110% and that you don't have the competence to reach even 70%. How does that sound? Not good, I imagine. But this is what happens again and again.

Presenters set themselves unrealistic expectations. They think *I have to speak like a native speaker, I have to make everyone laugh, I have to make people like me, I have to make people think I am the leading expert in this field.* Added to this, people hugely under-estimate their own capacity to deliver. They fail to see their own knowledge, their own expertise, their own value to the audience and the value the audience sees in them. Get real! You *are* competent and you *can* do a good enough job.

And remember: your English is good enough. As we said in the Introduction, non-native speakers are often far more effective international speakers than many native speakers. Effective communication is not only a linguistic issue. Force of personality, technical expertise and general clarity of communication style are often far more important.

### Get in control

People feel stress when they decide to give up control. However, taking control is relatively easy if you follow three simple steps.

### 1 Control your message

Presenters feel stressed when they haven't planned or can't remember three essential elements of their presentation: the objective, the content and the right English vocabulary. Taking control simply means effective planning of these three factors.

**Do** use English text on your slides to help you remember key points.

**Don't** try to memorise everything.

### 2  Control your body

Effective presenters have to manage their bodies. Like professional sportspeople, they should drink lots of water, stretch and warm up, breathe properly, relax and not waste energy.

**Do** go and talk to your audience before you speak – smile and laugh to relax.

**Don't** sit nervously and get stressed by watching people enter the room.

### 3  Control your mind

Working with your mind is one of the most important areas of stress management. Thinking positive thoughts about yourself, your performance and your audience is the way to say goodbye to stress.

Some positive thoughts to include:

— *I've got something useful to say.*

— *I can actually do this quite well.*

— *This is just a conversation with a few friends.*

— *The audience must be really interested or they wouldn't have come.*

— *This audience respects me.*

— *I'm not perfect, and I don't have to be.*

— *This presentation will be great practice. I'll be even better next time after this.*

**Do** focus on the positive in the moments before you start.

**Don't** allow one single negative ideas into your thoughts.

After your next presentation, ask yourself these questions:

— How much stress did I feel?

— Why did I feel stressed?

— What will I do next time to avoid feeling stressed?

After your next presentation, ask your audience these questions:

— How much did I look stressed?

— How much did I sound stressed?

— How should I avoid stress in the future?

You may be surprised by to find out that audiences are generally unable to tell when you're feeling stressed because it's all … in your mind!

**HOT TIPS**

- Be positive about yourself
- Be positive about other people
- Take control and say goodbye to stress for ever

# 30 Managing the physical environment

I once landed in a foreign city to deliver a presentation. I'd done the usual and prepared around fifty *PowerPoint* slides to introduce my organisation, its products and services. When I got to the room, I was informed that the electricity was off that day and would I mind using chalk and a blackboard (30 × 30cm)? I smiled and got on with it. But my lesson was learned! Effective presentations require planning and management of the environment.

**Prepare the room and test the equipment before you speak**

If possible, get information about the room size with seating layout.

Ensure that extra seats are available in case of a last-minute rush.

Check that there will be a screen which all the audience can see.

Ask about the luminosity of the digital projector – aim for 2,000–3,000 lumens.

Get there early to test your equipment.

Set the lighting to a comfortable level for the audience.

Take your own extension cables and adaptors.

Have back-up disks available.

Have alternative media back up in the form of handouts or transparencies in case of total disaster!

**Manage the environment with a colleague during the presentation**

Ask a colleague to act as host to latecomers so that they can be directed to seats quickly.

Ask a colleague to introduce you – choose someone with a sense of humour!

Ask a colleague to sit near the windows in case fresh air is needed.

Ask a colleague to handle any outside noise interference if it occurs.

A good host always checks if the guests are comfortable during the presentation.

*Can everyone hear me OK?*

*Is it too warm for everyone?*

*Shall we take a short break?*

*Can everyone see the screen?*

*Shall we open a window?*

*Does everyone have a copy of the handouts?*

**Deal with logistics of the post-presentation moment**
Be prepared for requests for handouts. People always ask for handouts, but I prefer to email copies of slides afterwards. Giving your email address to people creates a channel for further contact and, importantly, possible business development.

Make sure you have the time and a place to talk to people after a presentation. This may be the opportunity for important networking so schedule some free time after the presentation and know a place where you can get a coffee.

To maximise post-presentation networking opportunities, make sure you have a good knowledge of the local environment, which means knowing any scheduled events, good restaurants in the area and the travel logistics to and from various venues.

**HOT TIPS**

- Research the facilities of the presentation venue
- Check out the room and your equipment well in advance
- Manage post-presentation meetings as these are the moments to secure business opportunities

# Learning diary – non-verbal communication

### How to use your learning diary

This learning diary is designed to help you improve your non-verbal communication for presentations. Photocopy it and use it regularly so you can improve over the long term. Ideally you should:

1 Complete Part 1 and Part 2 before a presentation.

2 After the presentation, ask your audience for feedback. Get their opinions on the points which you identified in Part 2 as your improvement targets.

3 Write any comments from your audience in the feedback box.

4 Use this audience feedback to identify future improvement targets for your next presentation.

Finally, maintain this learning cycle until you can't find any more improvements to make.

### Part 1: What did I learn about non-verbal communication in this module?

26  Using your voice effectively ...........................................................................

.............................................................................................................................

27  Body language ...............................................................................................

.............................................................................................................................

28  Practice makes perfect ....................................................................................

.............................................................................................................................

29  Goodbye to stress ...........................................................................................

.............................................................................................................................

30  Managing the physical environment ...............................................................

.............................................................................................................................

### Part 2: Which three areas of my non-verbal communication will I try to improve?

Target for improvement 1: ...................................................................................

Target for improvement 2: ...................................................................................

Target for improvement 3: ...................................................................................

### Part 3: Audience feedback about my non-verbal communication

### Part 4: Which three areas of my non-verbal communication will I improve next?

1  ........................................................................................................................

2  ........................................................................................................................

3  ........................................................................................................................

# Multimedia visuals

*'A picture is worth a thousand words.'* Napoleon Bonaparte

The multimedia resources available to presenters are increasing. In the past it was all about the overhead projector and those rather complicated overlay techniques which were almost impossible to master.

Now we have the wizardry and ease of *PowerPoint* slides, with integrated video or sound clips plus web browsing and, if we really want, live links with people in distant parts of the world.

Unfortunately, most presenters abuse the opportunities available. *Death by PowerPoint* has become all too familiar across the international business world. In the following units we will look at how to use visuals to support presentations effectively without them becoming a distraction. We'll also see practical tips on enhancing messages with targeted and expert use of graphics and text.

# 31 Slide basics

Ask yourself three questions when preparing your next presentation slide:

– Why am I using this visual?
– What is the right content?
– What is the best design?

## Purpose

Visuals are not for entertainment value. They should make content more transparent and come across with greater impact. However, slides often confuse and actually distract from the spoken word. Let's start with some design guidelines.

## Style

The slide template – background and header format – is usually determined by the company. Therefore, the main issue is to manage the actual text:

**Size**   Recommendations vary, but 36 points for headers and 24 for main text works well.

**Words per line**   Six lines and six words per line; no full sentences where possible. Use your own judgement, but keep it short and simple.

**Font**   *Sans serif* fonts such as *Arial* and *Tahoma* are easier to read when projected. Don't use a wide variety of fonts – maximum two per single slide. Use bold for contrast but avoid italics – difficult to read when projected.

**Case**   Use a combination of upper and lower case; avoid all upper-case headings.

**Colour**   High-contrast colours make text easier to read. Dark text on light background usually works best. Don't combine colours which clash: for example, red and green clash, and are also a problem for the 10% of your audience who may be colour blind; select cool colours such as blue for backgrounds if possible.

Use single words to express the key concepts:

**Not this ...**                                     **... but this**

| Qualities of a high-performing team: |
| --- |
| • the team has a good leader |
| • everyone is very motivated |
| • the goals of the team are clear to all team members |

| Qualities of a high-performing team: |
| --- |
| • leadership |
| • motivation |
| • goals |

Use the verb consistently to start bulleted points:

**Not this ...**                                     **... but this**

| There are three principles of customer service: |
| --- |
| • deliver products on time |
| • offering products at the right price |
| • we promise to support with excellent after sales |

| There are three principles of customer service: |
| --- |
| • deliver products on time |
| • offer products at the right price |
| • support with excellent after sales |

Make sure your style is consistent through the presentation, and don't put too much onto single slides.

### Graphics

Use images which actually relate to the communication objective. If they don't, leave them out! Choose the image type carefully:

- clip art can look all too familiar and unprofessional
- photographs are great, but it can be time-consuming to find the right image
- business graphics such as charts and tables which provide necessary data are usually complex and difficult to read. Use highlighting effects such as circling to identify key information.

Use coloured text to highlight key content, especially if quoting from a report.

---

## Quality – a way forward

The current quality initiative from the Board states that all departments must seek to improve quality by a measurable 10% by the end of next year.

---

### Effects

Use *PowerPoint* effects wisely. Overuse of text transitions and sound effects is likely to annoy and get people running for the door.

**Bullet points** – reveal points one at a time with a simple entrance effect to avoid the audience reading ahead while you are talking.

**Emphasis** – highlight key text with colour, underlining or circling, not by using capital letters.

**Fun** – if you have any fun animation, use only as a quick warm-up or a wrap-up.

### Links

Increasingly, presenters link to files during business presentations. If these files really enhance the presentation objective, then use them. But beware of the difficulties below:

**Text files** – don't display documents which are impossible to read when projected.

**Sound files** – playing sound files requires a sound system in the room which works and provides the right quality for everyone present. Check the logistics in advance.

**Video files** – quality issues also affect any decision to use video. Remember, projected video can appear fuzzy and unprofessional if the recording quality is low. Test before integrating into your presentation.

**Web pages** – web pages are like text files, quite difficult to read. Accessing the Internet also depends on a reliable connection. It's dangerous to put your faith in technology for critical input.

**ASK YOURSELF**

Check through your latest presentation. How many of the above rules did you really follow?

**HOT TIPS**

- Use visuals if, and only if, they serve to enhance your message
- Remember – crowded and unprofessional-looking slides will reflect badly on your professionalism

**TEST YOURSELF**

Which rules of effective slide preparation does this visual break?

---

*Quarterly sales report – 2006*

## 2. Current status by Product line

➤ **Figures for main regions**

| Product listing | UK | Germany | Spain | Italy | US | Ireland | Russia |
|---|---|---|---|---|---|---|---|
| A541 | | | 1 | | | | |
| A651 | | | 2 | 2 | 452 | | 23 |
| B234 | 452 | | 334 | | | | |
| B445 | 2 | | 1 | 122 | 8 | | 34 |
| C234 | 462 | | | | 14 | | |
| C436 | 2 | | 2 | | | | |
| D112 | | | | | 1 | | |
| D231 | | | | | 43 | | |
| D456 | 219 | 221 | 52 | | | | |
| E45 | | | 1 | | 1 | | |
| E65 | | | 29 | | | | |
| E110 | | | 1 | | | | |
| F45 | | | | | 15 | | 11 |
| G465 | | | | | | 34 | |
| H33 | | | 1 | 13 | | | |
| J89 | | | | | | 1 | |
| J678 | | | | | 4 | | |
| K787 | 31 | | | | | | |
| M566 | 1 | | | | | | |
| M678 | 345 | | | | | | |
| R56 | 1 | | | | | | |
| S456 | 4561 | | | | | | |
| T56 | 2 | | | | | | |
| X565 | 4563 | | | | | | |

- The UK is having the best results so far which is very pleasing for both local and headquarter management. It is 100% above target.
- Italy and Ireland VERY disappointing.
- We expect some changes next year.

---

**Possible answers**

1 Generally, the slide uses too many different fonts with no clear logic to the size, capitalisation and use of italics.
2 The slide uses two types of bullet point when one should be used. Additionally, no bullet is required for the text *Figures for main regions*.
3 The information in the table is not clearly presented. The text is very small and it is difficult for the eye when reading to identify which product connects to which figure.
4 The concluding text is underlined unnecessarily. It is also inconsistent in that the first bullet point is written as a full sentence, which is too long, with the second bullet point written in abbreviated form without use of the verb *are*.
5 The use of *some* in the final sentence on the slide is not specific enough. A more precise analysis is required.

# 32 Better *PowerPoint*

Here are ten golden rules you can use to evaluate your *PowerPoint* slides.

## 1 Design each visual to communicate one major point

Think from your audience's point of view. When you display any slide it's essential for them to know within five seconds what the core message is. You should be able to achieve this objective within the visual, using a clear heading, uncomplicated layout and a few words of introduction. Review your slides for transparency.

## 2 Keep things lively

Open any newspaper and your eye is quickly caught by one or two headlines that attract your interest. Apply the same principles of headline writing when deciding on slide titles. In order to inject a little energy into the proceedings, why not use a play on words, a little alliteration, or even design headings as questions?

## 3 Keep it simple

The vast majority of slides are too complex, both in terms of numbers of words and of graphical content. After finishing your preparation, think again and reduce both the number of slides and complexity of content by 30 per cent!

## 4 Highlight key words or areas of a slide

For slides where you simply have to introduce a section of text – perhaps an extract from a report or a quote from a leading authority – highlight the key words from the quote, for example in red with a light background, to support the content you want to focus on.

**Quality – a way forward**

Our leaders must develop **international relationship management skills** to build **trust**.

Each leader has to develop a greater **range of communication styles** to manage **international diversity** more effectively.

## 5 Start well

First impressions matter. Make sure the title slide looks professional enough to impress an audience as it comes into the room. For the second slide, find an interesting image to kick things off with a little bit of fun. Make sure you don't use images which have culturally negative overtones. And don't invest more than a few seconds on humour before moving onto your third opening slide which explains your objective. Long stories that try to be funny generally end up as very unfunny.

## 6 Finish well

The final slides should be the most memorable. One of them should summarise the key points of the presentation quite mechanically with bullet points. The final slide before questions should crystallise the main message with a powerful statement, quote or image. But don't use old clip art to finish!

### 7  Postpone giving of handouts

Given the natural complexity of many business graphics, it may sometimes be necessary to provide handouts, as tables and lists of figures are often not fully readable when projected. However, avoid this if at all possible; audiences tend to spend their time reading handouts when they should be listening.

### 8  Create interest with variety

Audiences love variety and will not be impressed with slide after slide composed of header and the standard number of bullet points. Think of yourself as a film director and mix it up a little between 'action' and 'romance'. Build in sections of three or four slides which form distinct sub-units in order to provide interesting but smooth transitions for the audience.

### 9  Proof read

Check that your bullet points start in the same way. Don't start some bullet points with a verb, some with *-ing* and some with a noun, as in Slide A; be consistent in the use of grammatical structures, as in Slide B.

A

| **Relationship-building skills for international leaders** |
| :--- |
| • Has recognition of the important of social relationships to some partners |
| • Socialising skills |
| • Mentality is proactive |
| • Can win trust |
| • Synergy for diverse groups |

B

| **Relationship-building skills for international leaders** |
| :--- |
| • Recognises the importance of social relationships to some partners |
| • Has socialising skills |
| • Possesses proactive mentality |
| • Wins trust |
| • Synergises diverse groups |

Make sure that spelling and punctuation are correct, and double-check any data or references you include. You should also know the source and meaning of any data you put on a slide (for example, is the figure from 2005 or 2006?), because if you don't, you can be sure someone will ask you about it.

### 10  Know what is coming

Finally, print your presentation with multiple slides per single page. Put the printout on the desk in front of you so you can see which slides are coming next in the presentation.

**ASK YOURSELF**

Can you think of three more useful tips for preparing top-quality *PowerPoint* slides?

1 ................................................................................................................................

2 ................................................................................................................................

3 ................................................................................................................................

**HOT TIPS**

- Prepare slides, leave them for a few days and then review
- When you review, aim to improve at least ten things; you should be able to find more
- Ask for feedback on your slides from two people: one who knows the subject and one who doesn't

# 33 Working with slides

The transparency and effectiveness of a slide depends on how it is used by a presenter. Let's look at slide management during a presentation on intercultural competence by a management consultant.

**TEST YOURSELF**

Complete the extract with words from the box.

| firstly | highlight | introduce | give | introduction |
|---------|-----------|-----------|------|--------------|
| areas | shows | | speaking | finally | questions |

❛Right, I'd now like to [1]............ you to a tool for developing intercultural competence. This slide [2]............a report which is generated by a psychometric tool called The International Profiler, a web-based questionnaire with eight questions.

I'd like to [3]............ three things on the slide for you. [4]............ as you can see, there are ten areas, from Openness at the top to Synergy at the bottom. These represent the ten core competence [5]............ which the tool profiles. Secondly, you will notice that there are scores marked with dots marked by high and low. These do not represent competence as such, but simply focus. The tool tells us where an individual is putting focus, but not if they are really competent or not. [6]............, high and low does not mean good and bad. All scores, high and low, have both a positive and a negative consequence which has to be explored between coach and coachee. [7]............ personally, I have used this tool very extensively with clients over the last five years and I have found it very useful to develop people's international effectiveness.

OK, so my main objective there was to give you a very quick [8]............ to the tool which we shall look at in more detail later. Are there any [9]............ at this point? No? Then let's go the next slide which introduces a case study on using the tool. This will [10]............ you a clearer idea of its benefits. ❜

1 introduce  2 shows  3 highlight  4 Firstly  5 areas  6 Finally  7 Speaking
8 introduction  9 questions  10 give

**TEST YOURSELF**

Look at this eight-step model for using slides. Find phrases or sentences from the extract above that demonstrate each of the eight steps.

**Step 1** Introduce the content and objective of the slide at the beginning.

..................................................................................................................................

**Step 2** Summarise briefly the key points you will use the slide to illustrate.

..................................................................................................................................

**Step 3** Link to the first point with a word or short phrase.

..................................................................................................................................

**Step 4** Introduce the other points explicitly with a short word or phrase.

..................................................................................................................................

**Step 5** Give personal comment on the content to add impact/create interest.

..................................................................................................................................

**Step 6** Repeat the main point, which the slide illustrates, to close.

..................................................................................................................................

**Step 7** Check for questions.

..................................................................................................................................

**Step 8** Bridge to next slide.

..................................................................................................................................

**HOT TIPS**

- Navigate your audience through a slide explicitly
- Expand upon key words and data on slides with personal comment to avoid the danger of appearing to be just reading through the text on the slide
- Bridge effectively between slides to show the logic of the presentation structure

Step 1: *I'd now like to introduce ... | This slide shows ...*
Step 2: *I'd like to highlight three things on the slide for you.*
Step 3: *Firstly, as you can see ...*
Step 4: *Secondly, you will notice ... | And finally, ... does not mean ...*
Step 5: *Speaking personally, ...*
Step 6: *OK, so my main objective there was to ...*
Step 7: *Are there any questions at this point?*
Step 8: *Then let's go the next slide which introduces a case study on using the tool.*

# 34 Describing results and trends

Many presenters will have to spend a lot of their time describing financial results and analysing business trends.

Here is a short guide to the language and grammar required to do this. In fact, there are just five elements to master:

1  Get the tense right
2  Select the correct verb or noun
3  Define the degree of change accurately
4  Choose the right preposition
5  Analyse with reasons and results.

## 1 Get the tense right

You have four main things to think about:

- If you want to refer to a specific time in the past, use the the past simple.
  *There **was** a rise in sales in 2005.*
  *Turnover **rose** in 1999.*

- If you want to refer to the past without saying exactly when, use the present perfect.
  *There **has been** a rise in sales.*
  *Turnover **has risen**.*

- If you want to describe what is happening now, use the present simple or continuous.
  *There **is** a rise in sales.*
  *Turnover is **rising**.*

- If you want to talk about the future, use *will* + infinitive.
  *There **will be** a rise in sales.*
  *Turnover **will rise**.*

## 2   Select the correct verb or noun

Here are some useful words you can use when describing results and trends.

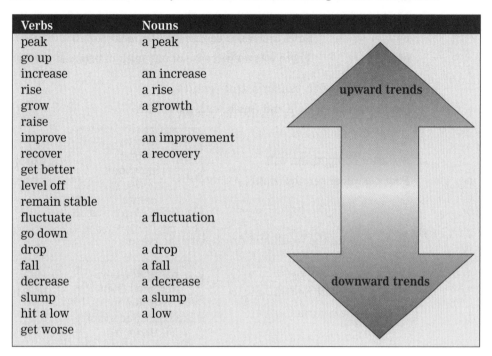

| Verbs | Nouns |
| --- | --- |
| peak | a peak |
| go up | |
| increase | an increase |
| rise | a rise |
| grow | a growth |
| raise | |
| improve | an improvement |
| recover | a recovery |
| get better | |
| level off | |
| remain stable | |
| fluctuate | a fluctuation |
| go down | |
| drop | a drop |
| fall | a fall |
| decrease | a decrease |
| slump | a slump |
| hit a low | a low |
| get worse | |

upward trends

downward trends

## 3   Define the degree of change accurately

Here are some useful qualifiers you can use with the verbs and nouns in 2.

Sales will increase
Sales have increased

| |
| --- |
| rapidly. |
| steadily. |
| gradually. |
| slowly. |
| dramatically. |
| significantly. |
| slightly. |

There will be a

| |
| --- |
| rapidly |
| steady |
| gradual |
| slow |
| dramatic |
| significant |
| slight |

increase in sales.

## 4 Choose the right preposition

| | |
|---|---|
| **at** | Sales stood **at** five million in 2004. |
| **from ... to ...** | Sales increased **from** five **to** six million in 2005. |
| **by** | Sales increased **by** one million in 2005. |
| **of** | There was an increase **of** one million between 2004 and 2005. |

## 5 Analyse with reasons and results

Begin with the reason and finish with the result:

| | | |
|---|---|---|
| Stronger competition will ... | lead to<br>result in<br>bring about<br>give rise to<br>create | ... a drop in revenue. |
| Poor customer service could ... | | ... severe problems. |

Or, begin with the result and finish with the reason:

| | | |
|---|---|---|
| The drop in staff motivation ... | resulted from<br>stemmed from<br>was due to<br>is a consequence of<br>is down to | ... bad management. |
| Winning the contract ... | | ... a lot of hard work. |

**1** Which of these sentences are grammatically incorrect? If necessary, change the underlined words.

1 Sales have increased <u>significantly</u>.

2 We have seen a <u>significantly</u> rise in sales.

3 This represents a large <u>grow</u> in turnover.

4 Sales <u>have increased</u> a lot last year.

5 This increase resulted <u>from</u> excellent marketing.

6 I think greater financial control could result <u>by</u> cost savings next year.

**2** Read this short presentation extract and choose the correct words.

❛As you can see, sales ¹*have risen | rise* quite ²*dramatic | dramatically* since the beginning of the year. In part, this is due ³*to | from* improved marketing. For example, there has been ⁴*significant | significantly* growth in our acquisition of new clients, which is very pleasing. You will also notice from these figures a small ⁵*reduce | drop* in business from the US. The sale of our Ohio-based subsidiary ⁶*is down to | created* this little glitch. Overall, the figures are excellent and I hope we will see a ⁷*steady | steadily* increase into the next quarter. ❜

**HOT
TIPS**

• Prepare financial presentations by writing down sentences with key results

• Add a personal reflection on presented results to liven up boring figures

**1** 1 ✓   2 ✗ significant      3 ✗ growth  4 ✗ increased  5 ✓  6 ✗ in
**2** 1 have risen  2 dramatically  3 to  4 significant  5 drop  6 created  7 steady

# 35 A checklist for visuals

Once you've finalised your next presentation, use the following slide review to check the quality of each slide. Make notes for specific improvements using the space for comments after each section, for example *Slide 10 has too much text – delete extract from financial report.*

---

**Slide review**

**Content**

Think about the following:

Is the objective of the slide clear?

Is the information on the slide the right information to communicate the message?

Is the slide confusing?

Is the slide interesting?

Is there too much information on the slide?

Comments ....................................................................................................................

....................................................................................................................

**Design**

Overall, how far does the style enhance the message?

How effective is the slide design?

- general accuracy (spelling, punctuation and any references)
- use of bullets (layout and consistency in terms of punctuation and grammar)
- lettering (size for header and body text)
- font (consistency and readability)
- use of capital letters (balance of upper and lower case)
- colour choice (readability and impact)

Overall, do the graphics enhance the message?

Overall, do the transition and emphasis effects enhance the message?

Overall, do the links enhance the message?

Comments ....................................................................................................................

....................................................................................................................

**Overall**

Impact: do the opening slides communicate the message clearly and with the right impact?

Variety: is there sufficient variety in slide design and content?

Coherence: do all the slides work together to communicate the message?

Comments ....................................................................................................................

....................................................................................................................

---

For very important presentations do the checklist in the following four stages:

1 Complete it yourself.

2 Ask a colleague with knowledge of the topic to complete it.

3 Ask a colleague without specialist knowledge of the topic to complete it.

4 Review the results and make the necessary adjustments.

**Ten top failings of slide management**

Try to avoid the following:

- overloaded slides
- illegible and inconsistent text
- too many 'seen before' cartoons and animation effects
- unclear or mismatched colours
- too many slides which are too similar to each other and too boring!
- allowing the audience to see all the slide text at once – no transition effect
- reading word for word from a visual with no personal analysis or comment
- talking without looking at the audience
- standing in front of the screen so that you obscure the visual from the audience
- relying too much on *PowerPoint* to communicate the message.

And remember, there is life without *PowerPoint*. There are flipcharts, overhead projectors, cards, pinboards and just plain old objects, all of which can help get your message across. *PowerPoint* is now very much the norm; those who do something a little bit different tend to be remembered and appreciated that little bit more!

**HOT TIPS**

- Prepare slides, leave them for a few days and then review
- When you review, aim to improve at least ten things; you should be able to find more
- Don't rely on *PowerPoint* alone. Use different media to create interest and impact!

**A final perspective on *PowerPoint* – do you agree?**

Edward R. Tufte is a professor of Information Design at Yale University. In March 2003, Tufte published a 23-page criticism of the application entitled *The Cognitive Style of PowerPoint*. Tufte lists a number of problems with *PowerPoint*:

- it forces presenters into a linear, slide-by-slide format, breaking data into fragments which makes it difficult to see the whole picture
- it leads to presenters constructing artificial and dangerously misleading hierarchies of information.
- it makes presenters oversimplify by reducing difficult concepts to bullet points
- it creates a barrier between speaker and audience
- it promotes uninformative or gratuitous graphics
- it makes presenters look unintelligent.

# Learning diary – multimedia visuals

## How to use your learning diary

This learning diary is designed to help you improve your multimedia visuals for presenting. Photocopy it and use it regularly so you can improve over the long term. Ideally you should:

1  Complete Part 1 and Part 2 before a presentation.

2  After the presentation, ask your audience for feedback. Get their opinions on the points which you identified in Part 2 as your improvement targets.

3  Write any comments from your audience in the feedback box.

4  Use this audience feedback to identify future improvement targets for your next presentation.

Finally, maintain this learning cycle until you can't find any more improvements to make.

## Part 1: What did I learn about multimedia visuals in this module?

31  **Slide basics** ...................................................................................

...........................................................................................................

32  **Better *PowerPoint*** ...........................................................................

...........................................................................................................

33  **Working with slides** ..........................................................................

...........................................................................................................

34  **Describing results and trends** ...........................................................

...........................................................................................................

35  **A checklist for visuals** ......................................................................

...........................................................................................................

## Part 2: Which three areas of my multimedia visuals will I try to improve?

Target for improvement 1: .......................................................................

Target for improvement 2: .......................................................................

Target for improvement 3: .......................................................................

## Part 3: Audience feedback about my multimedia visuals

## Part 4: Which three areas of my multimedia visuals will I improve next?

1  ......................................................................................................

2  ......................................................................................................

3  ......................................................................................................

# Closing and handling questions

*'Short-term memory is electrical; long-term memory is chemical. We can only do three things to increase the transfer of our messages from electrical memory to chemical memory: increase the relevancy of the message, increase the frequency of its repetition, or both.'* Bryan and Jeff Eisenberg

It is vital for speakers to end their presentations strongly. In the closing moments presenters create those final impressions, the real take-away value, so the message needs to be strong, highly memorable and absolutely focused on the main points the audience should carry out of the door.

As the Eisenbergs noted, we remember best those messages which are important for us and which are repeated often enough to allow transfer to our long-term memory. In part, therefore, the closing sequence of a presentation needs to allow for repetition, through a summary of the content; and a focus on the most relevant issue, the concluding statement.

After that, the questions from the audience will begin to flow, some interesting and some tricky. Many presenters find the questions phase difficult to plan for and difficult to handle. In the next five units are ideas to help you end your presentations with an effective summary and conclusion, and tips for managing the questions phase.

**36** Ending effectively

**37** Adding impact to the finish

**38** Handling questions: the RACER model

**39** Dealing with aggressive questions

**40** Taking a few more questions

# 36 Ending effectively

To end presentations effectively, observe five basic principles:

Be short        – you will lose impact if you go on for too long at the end.

Be consistent  – you will confuse if you start introducing new ideas.

Be clear        – you will be effective if you stress the main ideas in simple terms.

Be tailored    – you will satisfy your audience if you focus on their interests.

Be memorable – you will be remembered if you do something a little bit different.

With these principles in mind, let's take a look at how to build the final moments of a presentation.

## The signal

As discussed in previous sections, it's helpful to use signposting language during a presentation to help audiences follow you. Using a short sentence before you begin your summary is also helpful, for example, *Right, I think that brings me to the end of my presentation.*

## The summary plus reflections

The next phase is a brief summary of the main objective(s) and message(s) of the presentation. This shouldn't just be repetition of the introduction as this can appear to patronise an audience. Summarise briefly the objective(s) and key point(s), but add reflections. Stress key issues in more detail in a way not possible earlier. You can also draw upon any discussions or audience comments during the presentation to make the summary feel really comprehensive and to show that you have been listening to your audience. Look at an example of this last point:

> ❛OK, to summarise, I think that a decision to expand into Vietnam makes sense in two ways. Firstly, and you said very much the same thing in the discussion earlier, Sven, if we don't go now our competitors will establish themselves more strongly, which will give us problems in the future. Secondly ... ❜

## The conclusion

Do two things in the conclusion: firstly, stress the benefits you've provided to your audience; secondly, look forward to the future and highlight what's going to happen next, either in terms of things people will experience or things people should do. So, concluding means stressing interests and focusing forward, concisely and positively.

## Linking to questions

The final phase is to open up questions. This link to questions is often quick and easy – *Do you have any questions?* In more complex contexts, you may want to propose a sequence of topics and the types of questions to follow. For example, in international contexts you may wish to offer the possibility for everyone in the room to ask questions so that different subsidiary representatives can get information on topics relevant only to their local contexts.

Complete this conclusion to a presentation to call centre managers about reorganisation. Use phrases a–g below.

**a** Our job is now to

**b** the major objective of my presentation today was to

**c** firstly, we looked at

**d** what I'd like to do now is to summarise briefly

**e** So, in conclusion,

**f** This generated a lot of discussion and

**g** In the second part of the presentation

❝OK, I think that covers the last point if there are no more questions? OK, then [1]............ and then focus on next steps.

So, as I said right at the beginning, [2]............ look through the main options for the relocation of our call centres with you. We've seen the three options: [3]............ going offshore; and I think we agree that this is the solution with most problems, although offering the greatest cost savings. Secondly, there is the option to outsource the whole operation to a service provider such as CareCall. [4]............ I sense that many of you are against this because of the threat to jobs in the medium term. The final option, and the one which we all seem to favour, is to create a new service company of our own and run it as a profit centre. This preserves jobs but, as we have discussed, it will necessitate some cuts in salary.

[5]............ I looked at how to communicate the decision to employees with a communication plan. I think the mechanics are clear but be under no illusions that it will take a lot of hard work on our side to persuade our people that this is the right solution.

[6]............ I think we have a commitment to a new organisation which meets the needs you expressed and which the company has identified. And we have a plan to communicate the changes in the coming weeks which will support that new organisation. [7]............ communicate the plan and to communicate it successfully so that the whole project runs to schedule. I ...❞

• Remember, last impressions count
• Show enthusiasm when asking for questions in order to motivate your audience to participate
• Emphasise audience benefits and necessary action steps in the conclusion

1d  2b  3c  4f  5g  6e  7a

# 37 Adding impact to the finish

Concluding statements should communicate forcefully and memorably. As always, the style and content of the closing statements must be tailored to the type of audience. Here are eight techniques to make a lasting final impression on your audience.

## Eight techniques to finish a presentation

1 **Push to action**
Your audience should leave the room in no doubt as to what they have to do and when.

2 **Demonstrate tangible benefits**
Communicate in clear and simple terms what the audience got by listening to you for the last hour or so.

3 **Offer inspiration**
Get people walking out the door with some energy, ready for the next challenge.

4 **Achieve the feel-good factor**
Put a smile on the face of your audience with some positive news.

5 **Praise**
Acknowledging the fact that people have done a good job is a great way to finish.

6 **Emphasise creativity**
Sometimes change is painful, so appealing to people's creative instinct to manage the challenge can be useful.

7 **Play the team card**
Never lose an opportunity to do that all-important bit of teambuilding.

8 **Be a leader when the environment is difficult**
Model the right mentality with a confident forecast of success in difficult times.

**TEST YOURSELF**

Match these internal presentation extracts to the eight techniques above.

a ☐ ❛So, after this presentation you should feel that you now have the framework; you have the support and you have the freedom. You can now go and do the job that you wanted to do before you walked in here. Thank you.❜

b ☐ ❛So, the figures which I have presented demonstrate that the company is doing well. I should say doing great! And I hope that makes your Friday afternoon run a little bit more smoothly. Thank you.❜

c ☐ ❛So, to conclude, I have to say that these targets will not be easy to meet. The competition is ever tougher. The customers demand more and more. But I'm very confident in the people around this table and very confident we'll succeed. Thank you.❜

**d** ☐ ❝So, in conclusion, let's get out there and deliver. We've got a lot of customers who want our services, and who want them now. Thank you. ❞

**e** ☐ ❝To conclude, I want to stress just one thing. This project will not succeed without your support. And as a vision, today we start the project as a new team in Paris. And I want to end this project as one of the most effective teams in the whole organisation. Thank you. ❞

**f** ☐ ❝In conclusion, well, there really only is one conclusion. Everyone in this room has exceeded their targets so I have to say a very big well done, and please, do it again next year. Thank you. ❞

**g** ☐ ❝Remember, you are the best today. You were the best yesterday. Go out and be the best tomorrow. Thank you. ❞

**h** ☐ ❝So, looking back at the last year, I think we can all agree that change has been hard. But we've done it. We've restructured, we've developed and we've innovated, really innovated, to emerge much stronger than ever. The key to this was your energy and creativity which, I'm sure, will continue to be our competitive advantage in the future. Thank you. ❞

### How to create a high-impact conclusion

Remember, we looked at a number of techniques to create a high-impact opening. The same ideas may help you to prepare something memorable to finish:

- Finish with a controversial statement to wake people up
- Illustrate your key message with a fun party trick
- Find a great audio-visual to pull everything together
- Offer prizes to someone who can articulate the key message as a clever slogan
- End with a quotation from someone great and famous to illustrate your point.

**HOT TIPS**

- Plan something memorable with which to conclude
- Choose a closing technique which matches your communication style
- Practise your conclusion until you are confident and natural

### Inspirational ending?

Jack Welch, in his early days as CEO of General Electric, dealt with the need for major changes in the company's strategy very directly. He was frequently heard to finish presentations with a simple message to the company's workers: *Change ... before you have to.*

a2  b4  c8  d1  e7  f5  g3/5  h6

# 38 Handling questions: the RACER model

Many presenters get stressed by the questions phase because they're afraid that they may not understand a question or not know how to answer. After all, you can prepare what you're going to say but you can't really prepare what an audience is going to ask you! By using the RACER model below you will be able to handle questions more professionally and proactively.

The RACER model is a five-step process to handling questions:

**R** = Respond
**A** = Answer
**C** = Check
**E** = Encourage
**R** = Return to presentation

Let's look at all these steps one by one.

### R  Respond

When someone in the audience asks you a question, the first thing to do is respond. You have two main choices.

**Choice 1**

Firstly, you can respond with some form of feedback: *That's an interesting question, That's a good question, Thanks for that question.* Not only does this maintain a positive framework for the question phase, but it gives you a little more thinking time.

If you want to use a more neutral feedback phrase, you can say something like *Yes, I understand, Yes, many people ask that question* or simply repeat some of the key words of the question.

If someone asks you, *When do you think prices will increase?*, begin with a simple response *OK, prices.* It's a form of politeness and it tells the questioner that you are focused on their question.

**Choice 2**

The other form of response is asking for clarification. Doing this avoids the risks of giving information that does not answer the actual question.

Clarifying questions should become a reflex for international presenters with either a quick reformulation: *So, if I understand you correctly you're asking ...* or some form of more direct clarification: *Sorry, what do you mean? Are you asking about ... ?*

And clarification should not only be at the level of content, but also at the level of motivation: *Sorry, why do you ask that question?* Very often we need to know what is behind a question in order to give the right answer.

### A  Answer

The only advice here is to keep answers short, simple and focused on the actual question.

## C Check

After answering a question, presenters frequently fail to invite more questions quickly. As a result, there can be a rather uncomfortable silence as the audience realises the answer is over and people wonder whether it's all right to ask another question. Remember, the audience is the customer, the answer a product and so presenters should ask a simple checking question to see if the customer is happy with the answer, for example *Did I answer your question?*, *Is that OK?*, *How do you see it?*, *Do you need more detail?*

## E Encourage

If the presenter has satisfied the first questioner, it's time to move quickly, proactively and professionally to the next question with *Are there any more questions?* Sometimes, it may be necessary to direct questions at named individuals to stimulate the audience to get involved *Peter, you have strong views on pricing. Any comments on what I said?*

## R Return to presentation

If no more questions are forthcoming, move proactively on and return to your presentation, either to continue, *Fine, if there are no more questions, let's move on to the next section*, or to end, *Good, if there are no more questions, I think we can finish here.*

### RACER in action

**Audience:** Do you think customers will pay ten per cent more for our products?

**Presenter:** It's a very good question. My belief is that they will, if we offer added services such as I outlined today. But they won't if we don't. Does that answer your question?

**Audience:** Yes, thank you.

**Presenter:** Good, any more questions?

**Audience:** How are we going to tell the customer about these price increases?

**Presenter:** Why do you ask?

**Audience:** Well, I'm worried that if we don't explain the reasons behind the increases, just increase prices in the brochure, we will lose customers.

**Presenter:** Yes, and I agree with you. We need to define a very clear communication strategy to support this marketing initiative. But that is for the next meeting, all right?

**Audience:** Fine.

**Presenter:** Any more questions? No? Right, then let's go to the second point …

**TEST YOURSELF**

Highlight any phrases can you find in the extract on page 109 which the presenter uses to respond, answer, check, encourage, and return.

**ASK YOURSELF**

Write down two questions which an audience might ask you during your next presentation. Then write down a short dialogue in order to practise answering the questions using the RACER model in different ways.

**HOT TIPS**

- Prepare answers to questions which you think the audience might ask you
- Don't forget to clarify questions and check your answers
- Use the RACER model to handle the whole process proactively and professionally

Respond: *It's a very good question. | Why do you ask? | Yes, and I agree with you.*
Answer: *My belief is that they will, if we offer added services such as I outlined today. But they won't if we don't.*
Check: *Does that answer your question? | But that is for the next meeting, all right?*
Encourage: *Good, any more questions?*
Return: *Right, then let's go to the second point …*

# 39 Dealing with aggressive comments and questions

Strong and dominant personalities are the norm in senior management, so handling aggressive, hostile and confrontational audiences is an essential part of being an effective international presenter. How comfortable would you feel handling the following comments and questions?

*You're not telling us the truth here.*          *What you just said is wrong.*

*I don't think you have the expertise for this.*     *This approach is unprofessional.*

Deal with such comments and questions in two stages: firstly, investigate the real meaning behind what has been said; secondly, select a communication strategy to manage the moment.

## Analysing reasons for conflict

**Psychological insecurity**   Aggression often stems from psychological roots involving insecurity with aspects of personal identity. Individuals who are very critical of others may actually strongly fear criticism from others. They may also become unstable in the face of aggression so it is wise to handle them gently.

**Pressures and anxieties generated by the business context**   Business worries can place enormous pressures on individuals leading them to react defensively when presented with, for example, a series of change processes which will lead to job losses. Consider that their comments may be partly justified.

**Relationship failure**   Trust has broken down when individuals begin to question your credibility or trustworthiness.

**Difference of opinion**   Genuine differences of opinion are not only predictable but essential in the business world to generate creative insight. It is important not to lose sight of the positive value of disagreement or scepticism.

**Power play**   Business relationships are often driven by power games between individuals. It is essential to identify when this is happening in order to maintain personal standing.

**Communication style**   Internationally, what individuals actually term as conflict varies enormously. What you see as honest and direct feedback may seem aggressive and confrontational to me. Assessing communication style is always important in analysing conflict.

## Developing strategies for dealing with conflict

Conflicts are managed effectively by presenters who recognise the reasons for conflict, who stay in control of their own emotions and who develop effective communication strategies. When a difficult situation arises, a presenter firstly has to decide whether to deal with it during the presentation in front of a group, or privately in a later face-to-face meeting.

This is an important decision as working through real conflict may be painful and take time. However, whether handling things face-to-face or one-to-one, conflict must be first handled using the Clarify – Analyse – Recognise (CAR) process:

**C** Clarify what the person is trying to say to you
*Sorry, what do you mean exactly?* or *You mean that ...*

**A** Analyse the facts and feelings behind the situation with follow-up questions
*Can you explain a little bit more the background to your comment?*

**R** Recognise the other person's feelings and point of view
*Right, I see what you are saying. For you ...*

After the CAR process, a presenter must decide on a strategy to deal with the conflict. Here are some typical strategies to choose from.

**H** Hit back when people attack. Being strong in front of aggressive types is essential.

**A** Agree if the criticism, doubt or fear is justified. If you don't, you lose credibility.

**R** Reach a compromise to save face. Both of you may have a legitimate viewpoint.

**D** Defend when you feel you are right, but go through the CAR process first.

**E** Explain misunderstanding if that is simply the reason for the conflict.

**R** Retreat and avoid conflict if you feel a battle can't be won or is best fought later.

---

**TEST YOURSELF**

Now match these comments from a presenter to one of the HARDER strategies.

**1** I think there's a little misunderstanding. When I said this, I didn't mean ...

..................................................................................................................................

**2** Actually, I think if we look at things in more detail you'll see what I mean.

..................................................................................................................................

**3** OK, maybe we should turn to the next topic and come back to this later.

..................................................................................................................................

**4** To be honest, I don't feel that such negative comments are very useful.

..................................................................................................................................

**5** Perhaps we have to accept that we are both right on this one.

..................................................................................................................................

**6** I accept what you're saying and I can hear your frustration.

..................................................................................................................................

---

**HOT TIPS**

• Understand the reasons for conflict
• Take time to clarify, analyse and recognise
• Choose a strategy right for the person, the situation and the long-term relationship

1 Explain   2 Defend   3 Retreat   4 Hit back   5 Reach a compromise   6 Agree

# 40 Taking a few more questions

Let's close with a look at eight more typical situations which you may face as a presenter during question time.

1 **The questioner wants information and you don't know the answer**
   Don't say I have no idea. It's honest but not helpful or professional.
   Do offer to find the information at a later date if you don't know at the time.

2 **The questioner asks something outside the scope of the presentation**
   Don't just reject a question and make the questioner feel stupid.
   Do reject the question sensitively and offer to discuss at a later date.

3 **The questioner hasn't listened and asks for something you already explained**
   Don't sound irritated if you have to repeat information you already gave.
   Do use this as an opportunity to reinforce the original message.

4 **The questioner wants information about something you want to explain later**
   Don't lose the thread of your presentation by giving key information too early.
   Do give the audience positive feedback but postpone discussion until later.

5 **The questioner touches on a very political topic**
   Don't get drawn into sensitive topics or discussions.
   Do show diplomacy and give a balanced answer without strong judgements.

6 **The questioner is just difficult to understand**
   Don't guess what people are trying to ask you or you will answer the wrong question.
   Do take time to clarify and summarise.

7 **The questioner identifies that you have said something factually incorrect**
   Don't get angry or try to deny that you were wrong.
   Do thank and acknowledge the person for helping your audience get the right facts.

8 **The questioner asks too many questions and stops other people speaking**
   Don't end up having a long conversation with just one member of the audience.
   Do be firm and insist that other people should have a chance to ask questions, too.

**TEST YOURSELF**

Take a look at these presentation extracts taken from a briefing given to a project steering committee. Match the extracts to the eight typical situations on page 113.

**Extract A** ☐

Audience: Could you say something about the resource situation in Spain?

Presenter: Yes, if I may, I'll come to that in around ten minutes because I'd like to deal with Sweden first. But I will certainly deal with this.

**Extract B** ☐

Audience: You mentioned an investment level of €8m, I think the figure is €12m.

Presenter: Absolutely. You're right. I do apologise. €8m was the original figure but we revised this to €12m at the mid-project meeting. Thank you for clarifying that.

**Extract C** ☐

Audience: So why do we have this delay in Greece?

Presenter: Yes, it's an important question. As I explained a little earlier, the main issue is personnel. We don't have enough people and enough qualified people. What I didn't say is that we have planned a meeting in August to try to correct this situation.

**Extract D** ☐

Audience: So what is the projected number of users in the Italian subsidiary?

Presenter: It's a good question but, unfortunately, I don't have those figures with me. I will check and come back to you. In fact, I'll check and forward the figure to everyone tomorrow. Is that OK?

See page 139 in Module 10 for more useful phrases for handling questions.

**ASK YOURSELF**

Can you think of any more challenging situations which you find difficult to handle during question time? For each situation:

1   note down one 'don't' and one 'do'
2   write down a sentence you can use to handle the situation in English
3   get some feedback from a native speaker about your notes for 1 and 2.

Extract A: 4   Extract B: 7   Extract C: 3   Extract D: 1

- Anticipate questions by writing them down on cards before the presentation
- Rehearse answering the questions by placing all the cards face down on a table, turning them over one by one and improvising an answer to each
- Remember to apply the RACER model when answering questions

### Some final words about questions

Remember that the questions phase at the end of a presentation is a great opportunity to satisfy your audience by providing clearly and concisely any missing information which they need. Handle the process proactively, positively and professionally so that the audience walks out of the door with the right impression of you and your presentation topic.

# Learning diary – closing and handling questions

## How to use your learning diary

This learning diary is designed to help you improve how you close presentations and handle questions. Photocopy it and use it regularly so you can improve over the long term. Ideally you should:

1 Complete Part 1 and Part 2 before a presentation.

2 After the presentation, ask your audience for feedback. Get their opinions on the points which you identified in Part 2 as your improvement targets.

3 Write any comments from your audience in the feedback box.

4 Use this audience feedback to identify future improvement targets for your next presentation.

Finally, maintain this learning cycle until you can't find any more improvements to make.

**Part 1: What did I learn about closing and handling questions in this module?**

36  **Ending effectively** ....................................................................................

...............................................................................................................

37  **Adding impact to the finish** .......................................................................

...............................................................................................................

38  **Handling questions: the RACER model** ......................................................

...............................................................................................................

39  **Dealing with aggressive comments and questions** .....................................

...............................................................................................................

40  **Taking a few more questions** .....................................................................

...............................................................................................................

**Part 2: Which three areas of closing and handling questions will I try to improve?**

Target for improvement 1: ...............................................................................

Target for improvement 2: ...............................................................................

Target for improvement 3: ...............................................................................

**Part 3: Audience feedback about my closing and handling of questions**

**Part 4: Which three areas of closing and handling questions will I improve next?**

1  ..............................................................................................................

2  ..............................................................................................................

3  ..............................................................................................................

# Advice for key presentation contexts

*'The only thing to do with good advice is pass it on. It is never any use to oneself.'* Oscar Wilde

**M**ost professionals regularly make presentations but don't actually realise it. In reality, few professionals actually have to stand in front of a large conference audience and deliver a winning message over a ninety-minute period. However, many regularly stand or sit in front of a variety of internal and external audiences to deliver short presentations to initiate meetings and discussions. For example, many meetings commonly start, for example, with a ten-minute informal presentation on problems to be discussed or a review of results or clarification of project status. Many negotiations begin with a brief presentation of needs and a series of proposals to get the process started.

These are all presentation moments and require all the skills described in this book. This module gives tips on how to be effective in five of these common and key business presentation situations.

**41** How to present problems: introducing the issue

**42** How to present problems: analysing the challenge

**43** How to present the status of a project

**44** How to present to customers

**45** How to present yourself: personal branding

# 41 How to present problems: introducing the issue

Problems can generate conflict so extra care has to be taken when presenting difficult issues. This module deals with presenting problems in two phases. This unit deals with the first phase: introducing the issue. In Unit 42, ways of presenting an analysis of a problem are introduced.

## A checklist for preparing to introduce a problem

### Perspectives – goal and roles

Misunderstandings about problems often arise because of different perspectives and priorities. Before presenting a problem at a meeting it is vital to talk to people in order to check how they understand the issue, how they see their role in solving the problem and what purpose the meeting can play.

Failure to prepare the ground by not clarifying these issues risks wasting time and provoking conflict unnecessarily. Remember, if it's a serious problem, use the phone and talk to people directly before the meeting. Don't rely on email!

### Agenda and process

Your presentation should include a proposed agenda and process for the discussion with both format (brainstorming, round table, workshop) and analytical tools (SWOT, force field analysis) worked out. As with goals and roles, this has to be discussed and agreed before the meeting so that the introduction to your presentation simply documents an already-agreed process.

### Information + tasks

Your presentation of the problem will fail if participants of the meeting have not read and digested key information and/or completed key tasks. Again, this may need extensive pre-presentation networking to make sure homework is done.

### Schedule and venue – basic logistics

And finally, don't allow anything to undermine the good work you have just done. Ensure basic logistics are in place – drinks, refreshments – to create a positive atmosphere.

### Information – a culture warning

Remember – be careful not to underestimate cultural differences in relation to information. In some business cultures an in-depth analysis may be required before discussion of a problem can begin. In other contexts, a brief summary of the challenge may be enough before getting down to discussion solutions.

**TEST YOURSELF**

Have a look at these elements of an effective introduction to a problem. Then match them to the correct paragraph of the presentation. The paragraphs are in the correct order.

**Paragraph**

1 Review agenda ☐

2 Clarify meeting process ☐

3 State common objectives with commitment to action ☐

4 State roles ☐

5 Check people are happy with process ☐

6 Positive welcome and introductions ☐

**Paragraph 1**

❛Right, shall we get started? We have a job to do today. So, to begin, let me just say a warm welcome to Johan and Birgitta from Stockholm. They don't often join us so it's good to have them here, especially as we need their input today to find a solution.❜

**Paragraph 2**

❛As you all know, the purpose of the meeting today is to look at the quality problems we've been having in production over the last few months. Although we may disagree on details, I think we are all agreed that we need to take some form of action urgently. And today I want to agree on what action to take. In terms of process, and I have discussed this with everyone pre-meeting, Id like to give a short overview of where the main problems lie.❜

**Paragraph 3**

❛So, as you can see from this graphic, I've identified two major issues; low skills of staff, which is leading to mistakes. Secondly, there is the issue of the technical equipment. I asked you all to look at a report from our engineering team which has found that over 50% of the quality issues are down to technical problems with old machinery. I think this sends a pretty clear signal to us as to what we have to do. So, my proposal for the meeting is that we take these two issues – personnel and equipment – and devise an action plan for each.❜

**Paragraph 4**

❛I have asked Jane to give some input on personnel and I will deal with equipment. This should give us plenty of ideas to discuss and come up with some solutions. I hope this is this all right with everyone. Yes? Good. So, if I may, I would like to start with equipment …❜

1 Review agenda: paragraph 3
2 Clarify meeting process: paragraph 2, the last part
3 State common objectives with commitment to action: paragraph 2, the first part
4 State roles: paragraph 4
5 Check people are happy with process: paragraph 4
6 Positive welcome and introductions: paragraph 1

As you can see, the introduction to the presentation is energising, positive and clear at the level of content, roles and process. Importantly, this creates a constructive frame for the later analysis of the problem. Without an effective introduction, it will be difficult for speakers to move on to a more detailed analysis of the issue.

**HOT TIPS**

- Prepare for problem-solving meetings by clarifying goals, roles and process with people beforehand
- Do not rely on email for pre-meeting contacts – use the telephone
- Prepare a strong introduction to the actual presentation of the problem in order to create a clear and constructive framework for action

# 42 How to present problems: analysing the challenge

Let's move from phase 1 to phase 2 and examine how to present the analysis of a problem. There are many analytical tools used at different stages of problem-solving: some are specific techniques for identifying the actual problem; others provide ways to analyse and quantify the success of any implemented solution.

It is a good idea when presenting complex problems to international audiences to explain explicitly the tools and approaches used at each stage. This allows every participant to understand the methodology and his or her own responsibilities in the process. Failure to do so risks misunderstanding and conflict about the problem-solving process.

## How to analyse the challenge

Use the steps below to support presentations you make which analyse challenges.

1  **Identify the problem**
   It is common in business to use some form of process analysis in order to locate or highlight where the real problem lies.

2  **Analyse data to understand the problem**
   Data is then presented which provides an in-depth understanding of the problem.

3  **Investigate the causes of the problem**
   Some form of root cause analysis is then conducted to identify the causes of the problem. Cause-effect diagrams (fishbone analysis) are a common tool used at this stage to present analysis in a graphical form.

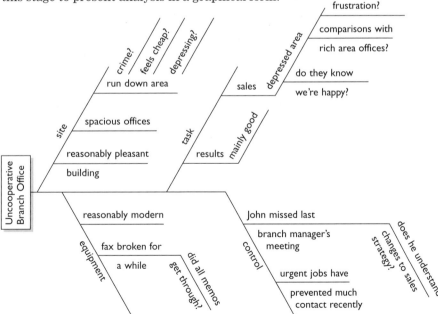

**Figure 1: Cause and Effect Diagram Example:**
A Manager's Analysis of Problems with a Branch Office

4 **Propose a solution to solve the problem**
Matrix tools may be used to evaluate and rank various options to solve the problem.

5 **Review data to check if the solution has worked**
Various forms of data – financial, quality – may be introduced to confirm the effectiveness or otherwise of the implemented solution.

6 **Introduce processes which will secure the solution over the longer term**
In this phase, presenters will focus on control mechanisms and the introduction of policies and procedures to make a solution sustainable over the longer term.

7 **Review the problem-solving process to learn from the experience**
The presentation will focus on harder issues such as the efficiency of tools and accuracy of data, alongside softer topics such as teamwork and a communication strategy to share useful knowledge within the wider organisation.

Your presentation should always state explicitly where you are in the problem-solving process, which tools are being used and why, and what is required and expected of the people involved.

How many of the above steps do you normally use when presenting the analysis of a problem at work?

How many of the steps will you use in the future?

### Focus on risk analysis methodology

Familiarity with risk analysis methodology is also very useful to structure the analysis of problems facing organisations. Risk analysis is an approach which analyses threats with a cost assessment of forecast scenarios. To present a risk analysis, use the following steps:

1 **Identify risks**
*Human* – from individuals or organisations, illness, death
*Operational* – from disruption to supplies and operations, loss of access to essential assets, failures in distribution
*Reputational* – from loss of business partner or employee confidence, or damage to reputation in the market
*Procedural* – from failures of accountability, internal systems and controls, organisation, fraud
*Project* – risks of cost over-runs, jobs taking too long, insufficient product or service quality
*Financial* – from business failure, stock market, interest rates, unemployment
*Technical* – from advances in technology, technical failure
*Natural* – threats from weather, natural disaster, accident, disease
*Political* – from changes in tax regimes, public opinion, government policy, foreign influence, etc.

**2 Evaluate risks**

The next step is to rank the risks. A value can be assigned to each threat simply by estimating the probability of any risk and multiplying this by the cost to the organisation if it happens.

**3 Handle risks**

The third step is to present a solution to manage the risk. You are likely to recommend either a change in processes to counter or insure against the risk, or some form of contingency planning where the risk is accepted, but measures put in place to handle events should they happen.

**4 Review the risk management process**

It is standard practice in risk management to review the risk analysis process itself periodically. Presentations here are likely to focus on testing systems and plans. Practise the above by analysing a risk to your business using the first three steps: identify risk; evaluate risk; handle risk.

**Attitudes to risk – a culture warning**

Attitudes to risk analysis vary significantly internationally. There are those who believe that detailed risk analysis is essential to prepare for action. Others may believe that such analysis is unnecessary, even impossible, in complex situations and that learning by doing is the way forward approach. Review your own expectations as a presenter, and those of your audience in order to tailor your message effectively.

**HOT TIPS**

- Tell your audience which methodology you have used to analyse problems
- If possible, get commitment to a problem-solving methodology to avoid conflict and misunderstanding
- Improve your knowledge of problem-solving tools such as risk management

# 43 How to present the status of a project

### Defining scope of the presentation

There is no such thing as a standard project. By their very nature projects are one-off interventions to change something within a specified time and budget framework. Consequently, project reporting varies enormously and depends upon a range of factors: the size of the project, its importance, the reporting culture of the organisation, and so on. However, many projects require regular reporting which is first documented, often in a single-page report, and then presented to the various stakeholders.

Typically, such reporting includes a summary view of the project in terms of major phases and deliverables such as:

Schedule – how well is the project doing in relation to the schedule?

Finance – is the project progressing well in relation to budget?

Threats – have any new risks been identified and are they being managed?

Issues – which new issues have arisen and how are they being handled?

### Tailoring presentation content to audience needs

Project managers often have a wealth of information in their heads. Their biggest challenge is to narrow the focus sufficiently for an audience which simply wants a quick summary with a solid overview which includes major highlights. Your presentation must offer information which is:

- objective and accurate
- clear and concise
- easily interpreted
- multi-level: you can drill down quickly from summary to details
- flexible: you can quickly show different impacts if any dates or values change
  tailored for specific stakeholders with specific concerns.

Use the above checklist to review the content of your next presentation.

### Which format?

Using the actual project reporting tool for your presentation may offer advantages over *PowerPoint* and *Word*. Critically, it will be possible to navigate through the different levels of data and project stages using the tool functionality in line with audience questions in a way that a linear *PowerPoint* presentation may not allow. Simply choose the format that will allow you to meet audience needs more effectively.

**TEST YOURSELF**

1  Match up each project word to the correct definition.

| | | | |
|---|---|---|---|
| 1 | ☐ stakeholder | a | a connected activity which affects the success of a task |
| 2 | ☐ sponsor | b | a result of a project |
| 3 | ☐ user | c | a back-up in case things do not go according to plan |
| 4 | ☐ sub-project | d | any person who is affected by or has an interest in the project |
| 5 | ☐ dependency | e | a task or series of tasks to support the main project |
| 6 | ☐ constraint | f | the person with overall responsibility for a project |
| 7 | ☐ deliverable | g | a limitation (potential or real) which can affect project success |
| 8 | ☐ contingency plan | h | The person who will work with the project outcome |

2  Project expressions: Which of verbs a–c **cannot** be used with project nouns 1–5?

*Example:* budget    a  to plan      b  to agree      c  ~~to open~~

(Answer: c. We can *plan* a budget, *agree* a budget, but not *open* a budget.)

| | | | | | | |
|---|---|---|---|---|---|---|
| 1 | schedule | a | to fix | b  to review | c | to face |
| 2 | progress | a | to do | b  to make | c | to review |
| 3 | problem | a | to solve | b  to address | c | to close |
| 4 | deadline | a | to do | b  to exceed | c | to meet |
| 5 | resources | a | to allocate | b  to make | c | to offer |

**HOT TIPS**

- Define the scope of your presentation in line with project reporting guidelines
- Tailor the content of your presentation to specific stakeholder expectations
- Choose a format for your presentation which allows you to move from global summary to real details in line with audience questions

**Project vocabulary – a tip**

Some international managers believe it is useful to create a glossary of project terms during a project lifecycle. Many key words such as *process* or *account* may have different meanings across national and corporate cultures. A glossary can help to build understanding and a common culture.

1  1d  2f  3h  4e  5a  6g  7b  8c
2  1c  2a  3c  4a  5b

# 44 How to present to customers

### Discovering customer needs

Customer-focused presentations begin with questions. We can only deliver the right information to customers if we know what they're looking for. But all too often presenters communicate on the assumption that they know what the customer wants.

International presenters with a customer-friendly mentality need to adopt a research-based approach which involves asking a lot of pre-presentation questions to determine client needs.

The questions which presenters need to ask in advance will depend wholly on the business context, but have a look at some examples which should be useful.

### Understanding the customer

Understanding how the customer sees suppliers:
> *Which suppliers contribute to your success, and in what way?*

Understanding how the customer sees the issue:
> *What challenge in your organisation makes you interested in our product?*
> *What are the underlying causes of this challenge?*

Understanding how the customer takes decisions:
> *Who needs to be involved to solve the challenge?*
> *How quickly do you normally take a decision?*

Understanding the customer's history:
> *How have you solved similar challenges in the past? With what success?*
> *Why have you purchased similar (or our) products in the past?*

Understanding the customer's expectations:
> *What kind of solution would best fit your current needs?*
> *What do you expect the customer service you receive to feel like?*

Understanding if you have covered all the angles:
> *What else do I need to know to deliver the right result to you?*

**ASK YOURSELF** What other questions can you add to the above list?

### Getting it right

As preparation for your next presentation, write down at least five key questions which you need your customer to answer in advance in order that you can deliver the right information at the right time to the right people in the right way.

## Delivering what the customer wants – a psychological approach

Behavioural science offers interesting insights into the broader issue of customer service. Here are some simple but important principles which can support the work of professionals when delivering customer-focused presentations.

### Get bad news out of the way early

Behavioural science suggests that we should save the best until last. If your presentation contains any difficult messages for customers to accept, perhaps issues of price or service, don't delay. Stating the negative issues early enables you to move on to more positive messages for the main block of the presentation.

### Concentrate the pain, divide the pleasure

Our experience of time is connected to the number of breaks we take. For the customer, smaller blocks of pleasurable experiences given over time will be felt as larger than just one long period. The Disney Corporation used this in the design of their theme parks by giving more, shorter, rides, giving the customer the impression of a longer, better, experience. For the presenter this means spreading out positive messages into a large number of bite-sized chunks.

### Get buy-in with choice

Don't limit the customer to one option. This makes it more difficult to gain acceptance. Allow customers choice in the product or service delivery. Highlight choices for your customer during your presentation and you are more likely to gain commitment.

### The same procedure as every year

Behavioural science tells us that people are creatures of habit and feel comfortable with regular, repetitive rituals. So try building up clear habits over regular contacts with your customers in either the organisation or delivery style of your presentation. Removing the disturbance created by the new enables customers to focus on your real message.

### Accelerate across the finishing line

The close of the presentation is the most critical moment as it is this final moment which leaves the most powerful impression. Ensure that you end with a personalised 'wow!' message which connects clearly to customer pleasure and choice.

### A final word on customer psychology

Don't forget to deliver on your promises. A presentation is often only a preliminary event for real action. Make sure you build customer delight by actually following through on your commitments over the longer term. Failure to satisfy raised expectations will lead to a damaging breakdown in trust.

**HOT TIPS**

- Before telling someone, ask them what they want to hear
- Respect customer psychology in how you handle positive and negative messages
- Never fail to deliver on your promises

# 45 How to present yourself: personal branding

Presenting is a little bit like communicating – we do it all the time. Every time we walk into a room we 'present' or represent ourselves. The suit, the dress, the haircut or hairstyle, the smile, the handwriting on the whiteboard, the way we speak and listen in meetings, the style of our emails, how we lead, the quality we produce.

All these actions present a package of values, attitudes and behaviours to others which we hope they will accept. Many consultancies now offer so-called personal branding services which enable individuals to manage this package, to re-package the package in order to present themselves in more effective ways to colleagues, clients and customers.

## So how can I brand myself?

In order to maximise career success it is necessary to establish a strong personal brand identity – a clear vision of who you are and what you offer – combined with a promotional strategy in order that you become visible and wanted by key decision makers. To brand yourself, you have to stand out from the crowd and become noticed, valuable and desirable in the eyes of others.

### 1 Define your USP (unique selling proposition = special features)
Brands are defined by their uniqueness. They are different and special. Pepsi, Nike, Nokia and BMW spend millions on defining their vision and values. Now ask yourself, what is it that you offer which makes you different and valuable to the people around you? What are your features and benefits?

Think about the following questions for a few minutes.

- What support do I offer colleagues?
- What expertise do I offer the team?
- What results do I guarantee to management?
- What levels of service do I offer to my customer?
- What vision do I have for my staff?
- Which skills make me different?
- What do I offer that others don't?
- What have I got that others haven't?
- What have I achieved that I can be proud of?
- What is my greatest strength?
- Which personal trait is most valued by others?
- What am I famous (not infamous) for?

Now write down a short brand statement for yourself – under twenty words – and read it back several times. If it doesn't excite you, do it again until it does.

## 2   Sell yourself

You may have great skills and personal qualities but, if nobody knows this, then you might as well not have them. Successful branding is based upon a communication strategy which means promoting yourself internally to colleagues and management as well as externally to customers and other virtual networks.

Promotion requires visibility; you have to be seen to be valued. So take steps to get known: get invited to meetings, participate in an extra project, offer lectures at a local university, write columns for magazines, go to conferences, build new networks and let people know what you can do. Start cultivating the reputation which will open doors and take you places. Remember, the best form of marketing is word of mouth. The network which you build – friends, colleagues, clients and customers – is the best marketing channel you can have. So nurture it carefully!

Above all, sell by leading. If you want to grow your brand, you've got to take initiative and assume leadership on different levels for what is going on around you, everything from taking the minutes in meetings to volunteering to lead new projects. You need to acquire influence in order to add influence to your brand.

### Putting it into practice

Imagine you had to present yourself to the sponsor of a new international project team in just ten minutes. Use this checklist to plan what you would say in order to introduce yourself most effectively.

1   Job responsibilities and professional expertise
2   Understanding of and commitment to the project aims
3   Experience of working on international projects
4   Positive anticipation of working in this international team
5   What you see as the critical success factors for working on international projects
6   Your preferred working and communication style in international teams
7   Personal interests
8   Family background
9   Common points you share with team members (professionally or general)
10  How you see your biggest value to this international project team

**TEST YOURSELF**

Match these sentences used by a project team member at the start of a project in Hong Kong to checklist points 1–10 on page 129.

a  I'm really looking forward to working with everyone. ☐

b  I like to communicate in a very direct and open way. Please don't see this as conflict. I just want to get the job done quickly. ☐

c  I'm responsible for IT support to our Asian customers. ☐

d  I was born and grew up in Italy, so I can speak quite good Italian. ☐

e  One of my great passions is sailing so I hope I have some time to experience the South China seas during my time here. ☐

f  I think the main objective of this project is to improve service to our customers. ☐

g  My biggest contribution will be my ability to speak Spanish with the Barcelona colleagues during the project. ☐

h  My own background in projects is mainly in South America and Australia. ☐

i  I believe project teams have to develop trust quickly to be successful. ☐

j  I think everyone has a lot of IT experience in this team and we all know the challenges of working internationally. ☐

Remember – the above phrases are suggestions only. You should always use language which you are comfortable with. Prepare some phrases using your own words and ask colleagues for feedback on your ideas.

**HOT TIPS**

- Present yourself to colleagues, management and clients as effectively as you can at all times
- Identify what makes you different, valuable and desirable
- Promote your added value internally and externally to support career development

a4  b6  c1  d8  e7  f2  g10  h3  i5  j9

# Learning diary – key presentation contexts

## How to use your learning diary

This learning diary is designed to help you improve how you handle key presentation contexts. Photocopy it and use it regularly so you can improve over the long term. Ideally you should:

1 Complete Part 1 and Part 2 before a presentation.

2 After the presentation, ask your audience for feedback. Get their opinions on the points which you identified in Part 2 as your improvement targets.

3 Write any comments from your audience in the feedback box.

4 Use this audience feedback to identify future improvement targets for your next presentation.

Finally, maintain this learning cycle until you can't find any more improvements to make.

## Part 1: What did I learn about key presentation contexts in this module?

41  **How to present problems: introducing the issue** ...............................................
.......................................................................................................................

42  **How to present problems: analysing the challenge** .........................................
.......................................................................................................................

43  **How to present the status of a project** .............................................................
.......................................................................................................................

44  **How to present to customers** ...........................................................................
.......................................................................................................................

45  **How to present yourself: personal branding** ...................................................
.......................................................................................................................

## Part 2: Which three areas of key presentation contexts will I try to improve?

Target for improvement 1: ...............................................................................

Target for improvement 2: ...............................................................................

Target for improvement 3: ...............................................................................

## Part 3: Audience feedback about my key presentation contexts

## Part 4: Which three areas of key presentation contexts will I improve next?

1  ....................................................................................................................

2  ....................................................................................................................

3  ....................................................................................................................

# Presentation language

*'The finest language is mostly made up of simple words.'*
George Eliot

This final module provides you with words and phrases you can use in your presentations. Treat the words and phrases only as a starting point. You will want to choose language which is right for you, your message and your audience. And you will want to adapt the language to specific presentation situations.

# 46 Language for the introduction

Review this checklist when you prepare the introduction for your next presentation. Plan which steps you need to include and decide the right sequence. Then use or adapt the specific phrases for each step, or simply use your own expressions.

## Welcome and personal introductions

Good morning. Welcome to …
Hi, everyone.
Let me just start by introducing myself. My name is …
I'm in charge of …

## Word of thanks

I should firstly like to say thanks to …
Thanks very much to …

## Positive framing

It's good to see so many here today.
I am extremely happy to be here …
It's a great opportunity for us today to …
(*Remember: never apologise for your poor English. This is negative thinking.*)

## Hook

To start, let me ask you a provocative question …
Take a look at this picture. What does it tell you about our company?
I'd like to start with a story today.

## Objective

The title of today's presentation is …
The target of this presentation is to present …
The objective today is to give some background about …
The main goal for us is …

## Personal introduction

Just a few words about myself: …
For those of you who don't know me, …
Perhaps I should just introduce one or two people around the table.

## Reference to audience context – with understanding and empathy

I appreciate that you have …
I understand that things have been difficult recently …

## Benefit statement

I hope this presentation will enable you to …
What I hope I will give you today is …
The real benefit I am hoping to deliver with this presentation is …

## Personal involvement

I'm very much committed to …
I really want to support …
I believe totally that …

### Structure

I've divided/split my talk into four main parts/sections.
Firstly, I want to …
Secondly/thirdly, we will move on to …
Then/next/after that/finally I will speak about …

### Audience role

If you have any questions, please feel free to interrupt.
I'd be glad to take any questions at the end of my presentation.
I'd like this to be interactive with discussion, rather than just a presentation.

### Logistics

The presentation will last around … minutes.
We will have refreshments at … and lunch at …
Are there any questions about logistics before we start?

### Link to start

OK. Let's begin with the first point which is …
Right. We can start by looking at …

**TEST YOURSELF**

Plan and practise the following presentation introductions:

* presenting at a conference on a specialist topic
* giving an internal briefing to colleagues
* introducing a new service/product to a customer.

# 47 Language for making things clear

Review this checklist to help your audience navigate clearly through your presentation with introductions to key points, highlighting of main issues, and explicit summarising of main questions.

### Opening
OK. Let's move on to …
Now it's time to turn our attention to …
Right, I think we can look at …

### Highlighting issues
I'd like to highlight three things on the slide for you.
I think there are two big questions to focus on here.
What I would like to discuss with you now is the important question of …

### Linking between a series of issues
In relation to the first point …
Concerning …
Regarding …

### Developing the topic
If I can just expand on that a little, …
It might be useful to give a little background to this …
If I can digress for a second …
One interesting thing, a little bit unrelated, is …

### Adding personal comment
Speaking personally, …
My own view on this is …
I see this as …

### Summarising main issue
So, for me, the main issue here is …
OK, so my main objective there was to …
In summary, …

### Offering questions
Are there any questions at this point?
Does anyone have any comments on that?
John, does that cover everything from your point of view?

### Moving on
Good, then this moves us to …
Right, now I want to go to the next point …
So, we should now take a look at …

**Connecting language**

You can refer to this list of connecting words and phrases when linking ideas and sentences in order to make your message clear, and to develop strong integrated arguments.

| | |
|---|---|
| Adding | *additionally, moreover, on top of this* |
| Contrasting | *however, but, whereas* |
| Exemplifying | *for example, such as, one instance* |
| Generalising | *normally, generally, as a rule* |
| Specifying | *in the case of, in particular, especially* |
| Conceding | *despite, although, even so* |
| Alternating | *alternatively, on the one hand | on the other hand* |
| Stating purpose | *in order to, so that, with the aim of* |
| Contradicting | *in fact, actually, surprisingly* |

**TEST YOURSELF**

1 Take three slides from the middle section of a recent presentation. Practise presenting the slides using some of the phrases in this unit to guide your audience clearly through the content and structure.

2 Now add five of the connecting words/phrases into your presentation.

3 Practise presenting all three slides again, using both the navigating phrases and connecting language.

# 48 Language for focusing

Review this checklist to help focus your message clearly with introductions to key points, highlighting of main issues and explicit summarising of main questions.

**Stressing explicitly**

I would like to stress …

It's important here to highlight …

I should emphasise that …

We need to focus on …

**Repeating for emphasis**

This has been a problem for a long, long time.

The more we discuss, the more serious the problem becomes.

We need to take action and we need to take action now!

**Positioning the core message effectively**

What we need to do is …

What is really important to consider is …

What we can't do is …

**Simplifying to focus**

To put it simply, …

Basically, …

Essentially, …

**Highlighting analysis**

Let's examine this more in detail.

What does this mean, exactly?

Let's just take a few minutes to look at this more closely.

**Waking the audience up**

Look, …

Listen, …

Let me ask you a question …

**Exemplifying**

Let me explain with a concrete example.

For instance, …

Just take one example to illustrate this.

**Emphasising with contrast**

In reality, …

Actually, …

In fact, …

**Rhetorical questions can add focus**

Presenters can exploit rhetorical questions in two ways to focus their message.

1   Use the question-answer dynamic which they create to focus the attention of an audience on important facts and arguments

| | |
|---|---|
| Timing | *When do we have to do this? In my view, …* |
| Costing | *How much is this going to cost? Well, the figures show …* |
| Forecasting | *What could happen if we did this? Our forecast illustrates …* |
| Reasoning | *Why do we have to do this? The main reason is …* |
| Allocating | *Who should be responsible? I think the best solution is …* |
| Meaning | *What is the impact on us? Let's look at …* |

2   Switch attention swiftly from problem to solution

| | |
|---|---|
| Problem | *This is the challenge.* |
| Challenge | *So how are we going to solve it?* |
| Proposal | *Well, I'll tell you. We plan to …* |

**TEST YOURSELF**

1   Look at three slides from previous presentations. Practise highlighting key information using some of the language and strategies in this unit.

2   Look at three slides from your next presentation. Practise highlighting key information using some of the language and strategies in this unit.

# 49 Language for handling questions

Review this checklist of phrases to help you handle questions. The R-A-C-E-R model you saw in Unit 38 allows you to manage any questions, using a proactive and professional process.

**R** Respond

**Positive acknowledgement**

That's an interesting question.

That's a good question.

Thanks for that question.

**Neutral acknowledgement**

Yes, I understand.

Yes, many people ask that question.

Right, …

**Clarification**

So, if I understand you correctly, you're asking …

Sorry, what do you mean?

Are you asking about … ?

Sorry, why do you ask that question?

**A** Answer

Here you simply answer the question which has been asked. Remember to keep your answer concise and focused directly on the question.

**C** Check

Did I answer your question?

Is that all right?

How do you see it?

What's your opinion on this?

Do you need more detail?

**E** Encourage

Are there any more questions?

Does anyone have any more questions before I move on?

Peter, you have strong views on this. Any comments on what I said?

**R** Return to presentation

OK, if there are no more questions, let's move on to the next section.

Right, I'd like to return to the presentation and go on to look at …

Good, if there are no more questions, I think we can finish here.

### Answering difficult questions

First work your way through Phase 1. Then select your strategy from the checklist in Phase 2.

**Phase 1 – Process**

| | | |
|---|---|---|
| **C** | Clarify | *Sorry, what do you mean exactly? I didn't understand.* |
| **A** | Analyse | *Can you explain a little more why you think that … ?* |
| **R** | Recognise | *OK, I see what you're saying. For you, …* |

**Phase 2 – Checklist**

| | | |
|---|---|---|
| **H** | Hit back | *To be honest, I think you're wrong on this.* |
| **A** | Agree | *I accept what you're saying. Perhaps I made a mistake.* |
| **R** | Reach compromise | *Perhaps we need to compromise a little here.* |
| **D** | Defend | *I think what I said is correct. If we look at …* |
| **E** | Explain | *Perhaps I didn't explain very well. I meant …* |
| **R** | Retreat | *Maybe we should move on and deal with this later.* |

**More question-handling strategies**

| | |
|---|---|
| Postponing | *I'm afraid I don't know the answer to that. But I will check and come back to you. Is that all right with you?* |
| Delaying briefly | *If I may, I'll come on to that subject later in the presentation.* |
| Avoiding | *That's quite a sensitive topic and I don't really want to go into that today.* |
| Refusing | *I'm afraid that's a little outside the scope of the presentation today. However, I am happy to discuss it with you after the presentation.* |
| Referring back | *Yes, as I said earlier, …* |
| Clarifying | *Sorry, I didn't hear. Could you repeat the question?* |
| Involving others | *Can I come back to you on that? I'd like to allow a few others to ask questions.* |

**TEST YOURSELF**

1  Write down five questions which you were asked during recent presentations.

2  Practise answering them using some of the strategies in this unit.

3  Write down five questions which people may ask during your next presentation.

4  Practise answering them using some of the strategies in this unit.

# 50 Language for closing

Review this checklist when you prepare the conclusion of your next presentation. Decide which of the steps you need to include and decide the right sequence. As with the introduction, use and adapt the specific phrases for each step or simply use your own expressions.

### Signalling the end

OK. That brings me to the end of my presentation.
Right. That covers everything I wanted to say about …
So, that's all I have to say.

### Introducing the summary

To recap briefly, …
To summarise the key points, …
Basically, we looked at three major points …

### Summarising plus

On the first issue, the key point I want to emphasise is …
Regarding the second issue, I think we all now see the importance of …
The final point was … and for me the big issue, as I said, is …

### Concluding

To conclude, I'd like to say that …
I'd like to finish by saying …
In conclusion, I hope that this has given you …
As a final message, I would like to ask you to …

### Final recommendation

It seems to me, then, that we should …
I would therefore recommend / advise that …
I think we are now in a position to …

### Managing logistics

I've got some handouts here which you can pick up.
Here's my e-mail address in case you want to get in touch.

### Thanking

Thank you for listening so attentively.
Thank you for your attention.
I hope that this has been useful.

### Inviting questions

OK. I think that brings me to the end of the presentation. Are there any questions?
Now, I'd be glad to answer any questions.
So, do you have any questions? Mr Nagamori?

### Creating impact

There are no standard phrases to provide impact. However, take a look at some examples below to inspire you to say something powerful and influential to your audiences.

**Calling to action**
> We now have to …
> There is no option but to …
> So, let's go and …

**Demonstrating tangible benefits**
> Essentially, what I wanted to give you with this presentation was …
> After this presentation you can …

**Inspiring**
> We've done it before and we will do it again.
> We are the best. Let's stay the best.

**Achieving the feel-good factor**
> And to finish, some positive news for you all: …
> As you know, I like to save the best until last, so …

**Highlighting achievements**
> Just to end, I would like to show you what we have achieved in …
> To finish on a high, let me show you …

**Emphasising creativity**
> The changes will require creativity and innovation. But we have the people to meet that challenge.
> We can find a solution because we have the most creative team in the industry working here.

**TEST YOURSELF**

Plan and practise the following presentation endings:

- concluding on a specialist topic at a conference
- concluding a short internal briefing to colleagues
- concluding a short service/product presentation to a customer.

Now add an 'impact message' to each presentation and practise it again!

# Learning diary – presentation language

## How to use your learning diary

This learning diary is designed to help you improve your presentation language. Photocopy it and use it regularly so you can improve over the long term. Ideally you should:

1 Complete Part 1 and Part 2 before a presentation.

2 After the presentation, ask your audience for feedback. Get their opinions on the points which you identified in Part 2 as your improvement targets.

3 Write any comments from your audience in the feedback box.

4 Use this audience feedback to identify future improvement targets for your next presentation.

Finally, maintain this learning cycle until you can't find any more improvements to make.

**Part 1: What did I learn about presentation language in this module?**

46  Language for the introduction ................................................................

......................................................................................................

47  Language for making things clear ............................................................

......................................................................................................

48  Language for focusing ..........................................................................

......................................................................................................

49  Language for handling questions ............................................................

......................................................................................................

50  Language for closing ............................................................................

......................................................................................................

**Part 2: Which three areas of my presentation language will I try to improve?**

Target for improvement 1: ..........................................................................

Target for improvement 2: ..........................................................................

Target for improvement 3: ..........................................................................

**Part 3: Audience feedback about my presentation language**

**Part 4: Which three areas of my presentation language will I improve next?**

1  ......................................................................................................

2  ......................................................................................................

3  ......................................................................................................

# Further reading

**CD ROMs**
*Business Presentations*
Jeremy Comfort, Patrik Schulz and Peter Franklin
York Associates
ISBN 978-1-900991-14-8
Available at http://www.york-associates.co.uk/info_pages/publications.htm

**Books**
*English for Presentations*
Down to Business Minimax Series
Bob Dignen
Falcon Press
ISBN 978-983-967251-0
Great resource if you want more English phrases and expressions for presentations.
There is an e-version with audio too!

*Business Skills – Presentations*
Anne Laws
Summertown Publishing
ISBN 978-1-902741-16-1
Reference and self-study for more advanced learners.

*Presenting in English*
Mark Powell
LTP
ISBN 978-1-899396-30-6
Good practical resource with tips for language and communication strategies.

*High Impact Presentations*
Jackie Stewart and Lee Bowman
Bene Factum Publishing Ltd
ISBN 978-95227-54-59

*Presenting to Win – The Art of Telling Your Story*
Jerry Weissman
Financial Times Prentice Hall
ISBN 978-0-13-046413-2
Creative ideas to transform your presentations

**Websites**
www.antion.com/articles/internat.htm
Articles on presentations

www.openmind.hr.com
Good for all sorts of articles – look under presentation skills

http://www.businessballs.com
Great site for all aspects of leadership, team working and professional
communication skills

# Conclusion

*'In my end is my beginning.'* T.S. Eliot

Congratulations! You have made it to the end of the book. As a result you will now have new sensitivities about yourself, about your international audiences and about the process of presenting. You will also have many more ideas on what you can present and how you can present it. But remember, sensitivity and ideas are only the first step. Now the real work begins as you start to transfer the input into your daily working life and the presentations which you have to give. This transfer will require effort and you will need to get ongoing feedback from those around you to ensure you can accelerate your progress as much as possible. I'm confident that you can do it. You should be too. Good luck!